LITERACY PLAY FOR THE EA

Book 1

Learning through fiction

COLLETTE DRIFTE

David Fulton Publishers
London

For Reinhard

David Fulton Publishers Ltd
The Chiswick Centre, 414 Chiswick High Road, London W4 5TF

www.fultonpublishers.co.uk

First published in Great Britain by David Fulton Publishers 2003
10 9 8 7 6 5 4 3 2 1

Note: the right of Collette Drifte to be identified as the author of this work has been asserted by her in accordance with the Copyright, Designs and Patents Act 1988.

Copyright © Collette Drifte 2003
Illustrations © Ella Burfoot 2003, Graham-Cameron Illustration

British Library Cataloguing in Publication Data
A catalogue record for this book is available from the British Library.

ISBN 1-85346-956-4

Also available in the **Literacy Play for the Early Years** series:

Book 2: *Learning through non-fiction* ISBN 1-85346-957-2
Book 3: *Learning through poetry* ISBN 1-85346-958-0
Book 4: *Learning through phonics* ISBN 1-85346-959-9

Cover design by Phil Barker
Designed and typeset by FiSH Books, London
Printed and bound in Great Britain by Thanet Press Limited, Margate, Kent.

Contents

Acknowledgements

The author and publishers would like to thank the copyright holders of the following texts used in this book:

Dogger, Shirley Hughes, Red Fox 1993
The Most Obedient Dog in the World, Anita Jeram, Walker Books 2000
Whiff or how the beautiful big fat smelly baby found a friend, Ian Whybrow and Russell Ayto, Picture Corgi Books 2000
Jack and the Beanstalk, Val Biro, Oxford University Press 2000
Guess How Much I Love You, Sam McBratney and Anita Jeram, Walker Books 2001
Handa's Surprise, Eileen Browne, Walker Books 1999
Morag and the Lamb, Joan Lingard and Patricia Casey, Walker Books 1992
Dear Daddy, Philippe Dupasquier, Andersen Press 2002
Can't You Sleep, Little Bear?, Martin Waddell and Barbara Firth, Walker Books 2001
Paddington Goes to Hospital, Michael Bond and Karen Jankel, Collins Picture Books 2002
A Letter to Father Christmas, Rose Impey and Sue Porter, Orchard Books 2001

I should like to thank the following for their support and encouragement throughout the writing of this book: Helen Fairlie of David Fulton Publishers for her sound suggestions and professional friendliness; Alan Worth, also of David Fulton Publishers, for seeing the book through the production process; Sophie Cox for her excellent copy-editing; friends and professionals who tried out the activities and made suggestions; the children's parents; and, finally, but probably most important of all, the children themselves. Some of them feature in the little scenarios but, for reasons of confidentiality, their names and details have been altered.

Collette Drifte

Introduction

Curriculum guidance for the foundation stage, National Literacy Strategy and learning through play

Many early years practitioners find it difficult to reconcile the Early learning goals of the foundation stage and the objectives of the *National Literacy Strategy* (DfEE 1998). The philosophy of learning through play is emphasised in *Curriculum guidance for the foundation stage* (DfEE 2000) and rightly so – it is beyond question that young children learn both more, and more effectively, through involvement in activities that are enjoyable, fun, and contain an element of play. The *National Literacy Strategy* (NLS) document outlines its objectives without touching on this in any depth and the practitioner may perhaps feel that it is a sterile document in terms of addressing the concept of learning through play. But the two documents aren't mutually exclusive and they can live alongside each other fairly well, since many of the NLS objectives do actually tie in with the Early learning goals.

For example:

Early learning goals from *Curriculum guidance for the foundation stage,* Communication, language and literacy:

- Enjoy listening to and using spoken and written language, and readily turn to it in their play and learning.
- Use language to imagine and recreate roles and experiences.
- Hear and say initial and final sounds in words, and short vowel sounds within words.

Objectives from the *National Literacy Strategy (YR)*:

- To use a variety of cues when reading: knowledge of the story and its context, and awareness of how it should make sense grammatically.
- To use knowledge of familiar texts to re-enact or retell to others, recounting the main points in the correct sequence.
- To hear and identify initial sounds in words.

James, Leanne, Daniel and Melanie share with the practitioner *Kipper's Birthday* by Mick Inkpen (Hodder Children's Books 1994). Melanie looks at the author's name on the cover and says 'That's "M" like "Melanie".' The practitioner reads the story, pausing occasionally to let the children guess the next word, or what might happen next. Later the children role-play in the Home Corner and plan a birthday party. They talk about how to go about it, then 'write' invitations and 'make' a cake, before having the party itself. In this scenario, all the foundation stage goals and NLS objectives listed above have been achieved.

Advisers and inspectors are recommending that early years practitioners give priority to the *Curriculum guidance for the foundation stage* in their setting, so the children should not lose out on either the stepping stones or the learning through play philosophy. As long as you plan your activities within the framework of *Curriculum guidance for the foundation stage*, you will still be addressing many of the NLS objectives when targeting the Early learning goals.

Some professionals working at the foundation stage, however, feel pressurised to teach towards the goals themselves, and are concerned that the stepping stones become overlooked. It is crucial that each child works at an appropriate level and is not pushed ahead too soon towards future outcomes. As professionals, therefore, we need to stand firm in our approach to working with all children at their own level, in their own time. By recording their achievements and showing why they are working on the current stepping stone, we will be able to illustrate the positive reasons for doing this.

Planned activities and appropriate intervention

A second debate to come out of the *Curriculum guidance for the foundation stage* is the principle it promotes of 'activities planned by adults' and 'appropriate intervention' to help the children in their learning (DfEE 2000: 11). Some practitioners feel that children should be left to learn through play, without any intervention by adults, while others may find themselves heavily directing the children's activities in order to highlight a learning point.

Most practitioners, though, would agree that the ideal is a balance between these two and the skill comes in knowing when and how to intervene, to maximise the children's learning opportunity. Leaving children to play freely in the belief that they will eventually learn the targeted skill or concept through discovery, assumes that learning is a sort of process of osmosis by which knowledge is automatically absorbed. This takes learning through play to a questionable extreme and will end up throwing the baby out with the bathwater – a child can play freely all day long without actually coming around to the learning point that the practitioner is aiming for. On the other hand, intervention can easily become interference – it can stifle children's exuberance and enthusiasm for the activity, because their curiosity and creativity are hampered by too much direction from the adult. This will never lead to effective learning. The practitioner needs to be sensitive as to when and how to intervene in the children's play, to help them discover the learning point.

In her book *Understanding Children's Play* (Nelson Thornes 2001), Jennie Lindon outlines the different roles that the professional plays when interacting with the child, including, for example, play companion, model, mediator, facilitator, observer-learner, etc. If you come to recognise which of these roles is appropriate to adopt in a given situation, you will go a long way to making sure children's learning is positive and successful, and fun. The skill lies in ensuring that structure and intervention are there in your planning, which in turn allow the children to determine the nature of the play.

Working towards literacy

When working to develop children's literacy skills, we need to bear in mind that literacy is not confined to reading and writing. All aspects of language as a whole, including speaking, listening, comprehension, expression and conversational skills, are crucial components of literacy. Without language, literacy skills can't be learnt. Speaking and listening feature largely in the *Curriculum guidance for the foundation stage* and so are acknowledged as the fundamental basis of the acquisition of literacy skills. While self-analysis and consideration of others' opinions are featured as objectives at a later stage of the *National Literacy Strategy*, children in the early years need to be introduced to these concepts. Paying attention to and taking account of others' views is part of the foundation stage work. Very young children have differing opinions as much as adults and older children, and they need to realise that opinions which are different from their own deserve to be respected and valued.

The reverse of this coin is that they should be able to develop the confidence to express their own opinion in the knowledge that it will be seen as a valuable contribution to the discussions held by the whole group. They must know that even if their opinion is different from others', it is a valid one and will be welcomed by everyone as an alternative view.

Imaginative play, creativity and role-play are also important elements in language development, and therefore in acquiring literacy skills. If we enable children to explore and play in imaginative situations, their ability to understand and enjoy fiction will be enhanced, as will their own creative literary abilities. Fiction and stories are, after all, only a different medium for expressing the creative play that goes on in every early years Home Corner!

Literacy (and language), as such, is not an isolated bubble or a 'subject' of the curriculum to be taught at specific times of the day. It cuts across every area of learning and is part of everything we do. While it is convenient for the sake of record keeping and planning to talk about 'Literacy', it's really something that can't be pigeon-holed or put onto a form with tick-boxes to record when we have 'done' it. It permeates every part of learning: reading the labels on maths equipment together may happen during a maths session, but it's still literacy; writing captions on the bottom of a painting links art and literacy.

So it soon becomes clear how using play, games and fun activities are ways we can approach literacy, enabling the children to develop the skills they need.

Who is this book for?

I hope that all early years practitioners will find something useful in this book and by 'all practitioners', I mean professionals who work in any capacity within the field of early years education. I have tried to use 'neutral' language in the book, i.e. not school-based terms, since the education of early years children takes place in many settings other than schools or nominated educational establishments. Although I have explored some of the issues involved in the *Curriculum guidance for the foundation stage/National Literacy Strategy* debate, this is not to say the implications are only for schools. I would argue that they affect everyone providing education for young children and so the issues are just as relevant to non-school settings.

But aside from this, I hope that the book will be useful to practitioners because of the practical nature of the ideas and suggestions. The activities can be done either within the framework of a session aiming for one of the official curriculum targets, or as a non-curriculum session with the setting's own aims in view. Of course, the activities are only suggestions, and practitioners could easily adapt or change them to suit their own situation.

What's in the book?

This book explores a variety of fiction texts and how they can be used as the basis of activities that are fun and contain an element of play, yet still have a literacy skill as the target. There are new titles and classics, old favourites and traditional stories included in the book. I make no apology for using some of the old favourites since there are always new practitioners and new children entering early years settings, who will discover these delightful stories for the first time. The veterans of the game will know that the children who are familiar with the texts never tire of hearing them over and over again, often knowing the stories word for word!

There are two observation and assessment sections at the end of the book to give the practitioner an idea of what to look for when children are working to acquire specific skills. These sections are by no means exhaustive and practitioners can 'pick and mix' the elements that are most useful to them, adding anything that they may feel needs to be included. I can't stress enough the importance of observation as a tool for assessment, since so much can be gathered of a child's achievements, progress and performance by this simple but extremely effective practice. The stepping stones in the *Curriculum guidance for the foundation stage* can also provide a useful guide to the child's achievements, particularly as the colour bands help to put the stepping stones into an age-related context. But we need to remember that they are just that – a guide to the child's progress en route to the Early learning goals – and not be tempted to use them as an assessment or teaching tool as such.

There are also some photocopiable pages which are linked in with the activities. They are not worksheets to be given to the children to 'do', but are a resource to save the practitioner preparation time. They must be used by the adult and the children working together on the activity, in a fun way without pressure.

What's in a chapter?

Each chapter follows the same format:

- Featured text – the title, author and edition used.
- Story synopsis – a brief outline of the story.
- Early learning goals from *Curriculum guidance for the foundation stage*, which are relevant to the chapter's focus.
- Objectives from the *National Literacy Strategy*, which link in with the Early learning goals.
- Materials needed – everything needed to do the session and activities.
- Optional materials for other activities – a list of resources needed for the other structured play activities.
- Preparation – details of what needs to be done beforehand. This often includes something like *Make a set of picture matching cards using Photocopiable Sheet 5*. The most effective way of doing this is to photocopy the sheet, stick it onto card and when the glue is dry, cut the sheet into the individual cards. You might like to ask the children to colour those cards that have pictures. You could laminate the cards for future use and to protect against everyday wear and tear.
- Introducing the text – for you as the practitioner either with everyone together or in groups, as you require. Although this section has been scripted, this is for guidance only and naturally you should present the material in your own 'style'. There may be questions asked and issues explored in this section which you feel aren't appropriate for your children's achievement level. The flexibility of the session means that you can 'pick and mix' those bits that *are* relevant to your own situation, leaving out what you don't want, or exploring further something that may be looked at in less detail than you'd like. (Note: There may be times when you prefer to explore a text together over several sessions and therefore you might use only a part of this section each time.)
- Focus activities – these can be done in whichever way you prefer, e.g. adult-led, in groups, independent, child-selected, etc. They have been designed to cater for different achievement levels and obviously you should 'pick and mix' as you require. You could adapt, add to or ignore them according to your own setting's needs. Some of the games have a competitive element in them, for example by winning tokens or avoiding 'elimination'. These can be adapted, if you prefer, to leave out that element of the game, in which case the children's satisfaction at their own achievement is the outcome of the activity.
- Other structured play activities – suggestions for other things to do as an 'optional extra'. They bring in wider aspects of Early learning goals and the NLS objectives, beyond the chapter's main focus. Some of the activities are competitive but, as mentioned above, you can adapt them to leave out this element if you prefer.
- Related photocopiable sheets.

CHAPTER 1

Dogger

by Shirley Hughes (Red Fox 1993)

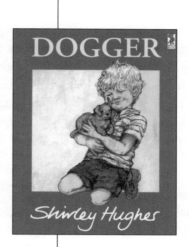

Story synopsis

Dave loses his favourite toy, Dogger, and is extremely miserable. When he sees Dogger for sale at the School Summer Fair, everything seems to be fine again, until Dogger is sold to someone else before Dave manages to get the money. Dave is distraught, but his sister, Bella, finally comes to the rescue and everything turns out well.

Early learning goals from *Curriculum guidance for the foundation stage,* Communication, language and literacy:

- Interact with others, negotiating plans and activities and taking turns in conversation.
- Enjoy listening to and using spoken and written language, and readily turn to it in their play and learning.
- Sustain attentive listening, responding to what they have heard by relevant comments, questions or actions.
- Use language to imagine and recreate roles and experiences.

Objectives from the *National Literacy Strategy (YR)*:

- To use a variety of cues when reading: knowledge of the story and its context, and awareness of how it should make sense grammatically.
- To use knowledge of familiar texts to re-enact or retell to others, recounting the main points in the correct sequence.
- To hear and identify initial sounds in words.

Materials needed

- ■ *Dogger* by Shirley Hughes (Red Fox 1993), if possible use a Big Book version and have small book copies available as well
- ■ Cuddly toy dog

- Flip-chart
- Marker pens
- Facial expressions sheet (see 'Preparation')
- The children's name cards
- Card tubes (minimum of six)
- Coloured pens

Optional materials for other activities

- Several items beginning with 'd'
- A selection of other familiar stories
- Sequencing story cards such as those produced by LDA
- 'Junk' equipment for making models for the Summer Fair
- Materials for making a frieze of the Summer Fair
- The children's own favourite toys from home
- Cassette recorder/player, blank cassette, cuddly toys
- Other books by Shirley Hughes

Preparation

- ▲ Make copies of Photocopiable Sheet 1 – facial expressions – (p. 9) for Group A.
- ▲ Make sure the items beginning with 'd' are placed around the room, in obvious positions (optional activity).
- ▲ Prepare the walls with frieze paper (optional activity).
- ▲ Record the story of *Dogger* on the blank cassette (optional activity).

Introducing the text

- Ask someone to hold the cuddly toy dog for this session or alternatively put it on a seat beside you as you share the book.
- Look at the front and back covers of *Dogger* and talk about the illustrations. Ask the children how they think the little boy is feeling. How do they know? Do they have a favourite toy at home? Encourage a few of them to talk about why they love their toy.
- Read the 'blurb' on the back cover and talk about it. Who is Dave? Who is Dogger? Why is Dogger called Dogger? Does anybody know what 'desolate' means? What's a garden fête? Has anyone been to one? What other names do the children know for a garden fête? For example, summer fair, summer fête, garden fair, etc.
- Share the story together, pointing to the text as you read. Pause occasionally and encourage the children to guess what the next word(s) might be. When you have finished, spend a few moments talking about the story. Do the children know how Dave felt at different stages in the story? For example, at the beginning, at teatime, at bedtime, during the night, during the Summer Fair, when he found Dogger on the stall, when Dogger was sold, when Bella swapped her bear for Dogger and when Dave went to bed that night.
- Ask the children to name some 'feeling words' – you could give them a start by reminding them of some of Dave's feelings in the story. Enjoy making faces to show the different emotions. Encourage some of the children to draw a face on the flip-chart showing each feeling word. Make this fun!
- Do the children like this story? Encourage them to tell you why or why not. Were there any parts that made them feel sad, happy, scared, worried, etc.? What other feelings did they experience while listening to the story? Can they tell you why they felt these emotions?

Focus activities

Group A: Give the children copies of Photocopiable Sheet 1. Talk about each emotion and then encourage the children to complete each face to express the emotion word underneath it. Alternatively, the children could take turns to pose or model their own face to express that emotion while the others draw it. This will create more giggling than anything else!

Group B: Allocate roles to the children and ask them to act the story of *Dogger*. Give one child the part of Dogger. Before beginning, spend a few minutes discussing how Dogger might have felt at being lost, sold and then returned to Dave. Do they act their play in sequence? When they have finished, give them the small books and let them follow the text while you read the story again from the Big Book. Are they confident enough to give a performance of their play for the whole group?

Group C: Talk about the phonemes at the beginning of 'Dogger' and 'Dave'. Do any of the children's names start with 'D'? Look at the children's name cards and decide which begin with 'D'. If none begin with 'D' can the children think of some? For example, Daniel, Derek, Daisy or Denise. Have some fun making up alliterative sentences with 'd' as the main phoneme: 'Daisy dances daintily on a dandelion' or 'Daniel dropped into a dark dungeon'.

Group D: Using the card tubes, together make finger puppets of Dave, Dogger, Bella, Mum, Dad, Joe and, if possible, some 'extras' for the Summer Fair. Draw and colour the features of each character on the tubes. Help the children to make up a play about how Dogger got lost and reunited with Dave, using the finger puppets.

Group E: Make a second-hand toy stall like the one Dogger was sold from. Let the children make the labels and price tags for the toys – you may have to help them and/or scribe for them. Help them to extend their vocabulary by using words connected with the stall: 'expensive', 'cheap', 'buy', 'sell', 'change' (money), 'spend' and so on.

Group F: Using the cuddly toy dog as Dogger, play a game of 'Hide and Seek', where each child takes a turn at hiding the toy and the others have to find it. Encourage the 'hider' to use preposition words as clues for the 'seekers', such as ' near', 'close', 'far away', etc.

Other structured play activities

- Make a School Summer Fair. Together, look at *Dogger* again for ideas about the activities and stalls that the children might make for their Fair. Take time together to discuss and plan the layout. Let the children use as many different media as possible to make the things for the stalls. For example, plasticine, papier mâché, building blocks, boxes and cartons, dried foods and so on. Use the opportunity to work on simple money exchanges, numbers, practising some of the races in the hall or yard, choosing or designing and making fancy dress costumes for a parade.

- Ask the children to bring into school one of their own favourite toys – make sure they're really 'second favourite' toys by checking with parents and that they are not part of crucial routines at home, to avoid a 'Dave-at-bedtime-without-Dogger' situation! Work in smaller groups and talk about the toys: what they are, how the children play with them, why they love them so much, where they got them from, what they are made from and what they look like. Record their comments on tape. Encourage the children to paint a large picture of their own toys and make a wall display of the paintings. Help each child to write a label or caption for the picture. Let the children play the recording of their comments while they look at the display.

- Play a game of 'I Spy', looking for things that begin with 'd' in the room. Ask the children to collect any 'd' objects they can find and display them. Play 'I Spy' against the clock, seeing how many 'd' items the children can spot in one minute, two minutes, thirty seconds, etc. Can the children think of other 'd' words, not necessarily objects, for example, 'Daddy' or 'do'?

- Make a large frieze of Dave's School Summer Fair, using the double-page picture in *Dogger* as the basis. Before starting, discuss with the children the layout of the Fair in the picture and how it will relate to the frieze. Plan together how to transfer the stalls and games to the frieze. Encourage the children to suggest, experiment and predict, try out and then rethink if their ideas don't work out.

- Have some fun role-playing other familiar stories. Make sure the children are certain of the correct sequence and then experiment with the story out of order. How does it change the story? You could start by using traditional stories such as fairy-tales and then play around with other modern but familiar and popular stories used in the setting.

- Let the children play with sequencing story cards. Have some fun arranging them out of sequence and telling nonsense stories from the new (random) order. Use a stopwatch or egg timer to see how quickly the children can put the story back into the correct sequence.

- Leave the cassette player, recorded cassette and the book (if possible, several copies) in a corner and let the children listen to the story again, following the text, in their own time. You could also leave several cuddly toys there for the children to snuggle while listening to the story.

- Choose and leave out other books by Shirley Hughes for the children to explore on their own. You could record some of the stories for the children to listen to while following the text. Alternatively, leave out other books about children and their toys or pets, and let the children explore these in their own time.

sad

happy

scared

tired

worried

mixed up

CHAPTER 2

The Most Obedient Dog in the World

by Anita Jeram (Walker Books 2000)

> **Story synopsis**
>
> Harry tells the most obedient dog in the world to 'Sit' and wait until he comes back. Harry is away for such a long time that the most obedient dog is visited by a bird, other dogs who tempt him to play, rain, thunder and lightning, a hailstorm, people passing and eventually a cat. This is the final straw, and the most obedient dog in the world is just about to go for the feline tempter when Harry comes back. The most obedient dog gets his reward by going with Harry and the family to the beach and having fun.

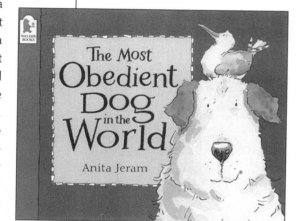

Early learning goals from *Curriculum guidance for the foundation stage*, Communication, language and literacy:

- Sustain attentive listening, responding to what they have heard by relevant comments, questions or actions.
- Extend their vocabulary, exploring the meanings and sounds of new words.
- Link sound to letters, naming and sounding the letters of the alphabet.
- Show an understanding of the elements of stories, such as main character, sequence of events, and openings...

Objectives from the *National Literacy Strategy (YR)*:

- To learn new words from their reading and shared experiences.
- To learn alphabetic and phonic knowledge through sounding and naming each letter of the alphabet.
- To be aware of story structures, e.g. actions/reactions, consequences and the ways that stories are built up and concluded.

Materials needed

- *The Most Obedient Dog in the World* by Anita Jeram (Walker Books 2000)
- Flip-chart, marker pens in different colours (washable)
- Stopwatch or egg timer
- Card, glue, laminator, scissors or guillotine
- Dog cards (see 'Preparation')
- Feely bag
- Birds' feathers, fur fabric, glue, scissors, paper
- Weather cards (see 'Preparation')
- Paper, coloured markers, pens
- Old yellow sheet, old blue sheet, beach toys
- Bone cards (see 'Preparation')

Optional materials for other activities

- Cassette recorder/player, blank cassette, soft toy dogs or other cuddly toys
- Other texts by Anita Jeram, published by Walker Books: *It Was Jake!* (1992); *Bunny My Honey* (2000); *All Together Now* (2001); *Contrary Mary* (1997)
- Lollipop sticks, card, glue, marker pens, scissors

Preparation

▲ Make dog cards: stick Photocopiable Sheet 2 (p. 14) onto card and laminate it. Cut it into the individual cards; make enough cards for twice the number of children in Group A. Using a washable marker pen (to enable you to reuse the cards) write a letter on each dog's tummy – choose the letters you want the children to learn. Put the cards into the feely bag.

▲ Make enough copies of Photocopiable Sheet 3 (p. 15) for each child in Group C. Stick the sheets onto card and cut them into the individual weather cards. (You could laminate them for future use.)

▲ Make bone cards: stick several copies of Photocopiable Sheet 4 (p. 16) onto card and laminate them. Cut out the individual bones. You can make them into dominoes by writing a letter at each end of the bone, making sure they will all match up. You can also make them into pelmanism cards by writing the same letter on pairs of bones. Use a washable marker pen so you can reuse the cards with different letters.

Introducing the text

- Before you read the title, look at the cover together and ask the children whether they think the book is about the dog or the bird. Can they give you a reason for their answer? Does the bird give them a clue about where this story might be set? Have any of the children seen birds like this? Where? Encourage them to help you read the title. Do they know what 'obedient' means? Where have they heard the word before? Do they know anyone or anything else that's obedient besides a dog? Are they obedient(!)? Who for?

- Read the story to the children, letting them see the text and the illustrations. Track the text with your finger as you read, being careful not to lag behind or go ahead, i.e. point to each word as you read it. Stop from time to time (for example, when the other dogs try to tempt the most obedient dog to play, or when the thunderstorm takes place) and ask the children what they think will happen next. When you have finished, ask the children whether they enjoyed the story. Can they tell you why or why not? Did it end as they expected?

- Explore the book together in more detail. How does the weather change through the story? At what time of year do the children think the story is set? Where do they think the bird went when the rain began to fall? What's a thunderstorm like? What happens when lightning flashes? Have they seen hailstones? What do they know about them? Why do they think Harry stayed where he was throughout the storm? What were the other dogs trying to make the most obedient dog do? Why did they get bored and go away? What do the children think the most obedient dog wanted to do to the cat? Are there any words that the children didn't understand? Help them to work out the meanings from the context.

- Who do the children think is the most important character in the story? Can they tell you why? Do they like the way the story starts? Can they say why or why not? Do they think stories that start 'Once upon a time' are better? Can they say why or why not? What's the first important thing to happen in the story of the most obedient dog in the world? What comes next? How does the story finish? Can the children tell you what might have happened if Harry hadn't come along near the end? Do they like the way the story ends? Can they say why or why not? Can they think of another ending?

- Spend a few minutes together looking carefully at the illustrations. Can the children guess how the dog feels at different stages in the story, by looking at the expressions on his face? What does the dog think about the thunderstorm? How do the children know? How do they think the dog got out from under the pile of hailstones? Why are two dogs from the group pulling a scarf between them? Which dog finally gets the scarf? Where do the children think he might be taking it? Can they suggest why two of the dogs are going into the nearby garden? Why is the grey and white dog leaning into the gutter? Do the children think that the most obedient dog would like to join in with the others? Why can't he? Why is the cat's fur standing on end when it spots the most obedient dog? Do the children think that the dog would have chased the cat if Harry hadn't said 'Leave that cat'? Can they say why or why not? How does the most obedient dog feel at the end of the story? How do the children know?

- What does Harry's name begin with? Are there any children in the group who are called Harry? Does anyone's name also begin with 'H'? What other names do they know beginning with 'H'? For example, Hannah, Henry, Hilary, Hugh, Hugo and Helen. Do the children know of any animals that begin with 'h'? For example, hedgehog or hippopotamus. Can they tell you *any* word that begins with 'h'? According to achievement level, let the children come to the flip-chart and write the words themselves, or scribe the words for them. Highlight the 'h' in a different colour. (You can make a game of this where the children have to work against a stopwatch or egg timer. Play it several times over a few sessions and challenge them to beat their own record.)

Focus activities

Group A: Let the group play a game with the dog cards and feely bag, where each child takes a card from the bag and reads the letter on its tummy before giving it a name beginning with that letter. If the children can't think of a name, can they tell you any word beginning with that letter?

Group B: Help the children to make collages of the most obedient dog and his bird friend, using the fur fabric and feathers. Let them choose a name for the dog and the bird and help them to label their collages.

Group C: Give each child a set of weather cards. If necessary, talk about them for a few minutes to make sure the children know what each one represents. Ask them to put the cards into the sequence of the weather changes in *The Most Obedient Dog in the World*. Let the children refer to the book if they want to jog their memories.

Group D: Ask the children to draw a portrait of their pet, or if they don't have one, a pet they would like to have or they could choose one of the animals featured in *The Most Obedient Dog in the World*. Encourage them to write a label, caption or sentence for their portrait, according to achievement level. Make a gallery of the children's portraits.

Group E: Make a 'life-size' beach with the children for imaginative play, using the yellow sheet for the sand and the blue sheet for the sea. Stock it with the beach toys and leave it for the children to play in when they wish. Take some photographs of the children playing on the 'beach' and ask them to help you write some captions for the photo display. Alternatively, you could make the beach in miniature in the sand tray.

Group F: Let the children play dominoes or pelmanism with the bone cards.

Other structured play activities

- Play a form of 'Simon Says' with the children, replacing it with 'Harry says' and instructions such as 'Sit down', 'Stay', 'Come *x* steps' (e.g. 2, 3 or 4), 'Wag your tail', 'Scratch your head' and so on. Whoever wins is the most obedient dog in the world!

- Have a free discussion about the children's own pets. Which is the most popular pet? Are there any unusual pets? How do the children look after their pets? If any of the children don't have a pet, encourage them to tell you about a pet they would like to have. You could use this as an opportunity to teach the children about responsible pet ownership, such as keeping the pet clean, making sure it visits the vet regularly for vaccination, worming and flea treatment, training it to behave sociably, clearing up the pet's mess, especially if this happens in a public place, etc.

- Leave the cassette player, recorded cassette and the book (if possible, several copies) in a corner and let the children listen to the story again, following the text, in their own time. Leave out some cuddly toys (if possible, different dogs) for the children to snuggle while listening to the story.

- Arrange visits to the setting by different types of working dog and their handlers, e.g. police dog, guide dog for the blind, airport/dock sniffer dog, hearing dog, Pets as Therapy dog and so on. Encourage the children to ask the handler questions about the work the dog has to do, about its training and whether there's anything special or different about the way it has to be treated. (Find out whether any of the children have an allergy to dogs and ask advice from their parents about how to manage the situation.)

- Choose other books by Anita Jeram and leave them out for the children to explore on their own. You could record some of the stories for the children to listen to while following the text.

- Arrange a visit by the children to a Pets' Corner, a pet shop or an animal sanctuary. (Find out whether any of the children have an allergy to animals and ask advice from their parents about how to manage the situation.)

- Help the children to draw and colour outlines of Harry, the most obedient dog, the cat, the bird, the other dogs and several of the passers-by on the card. Cut them out and glue them onto the lollipop sticks. Help the children to make up and write a play script about the story and to practise a performance of their play using the puppets.

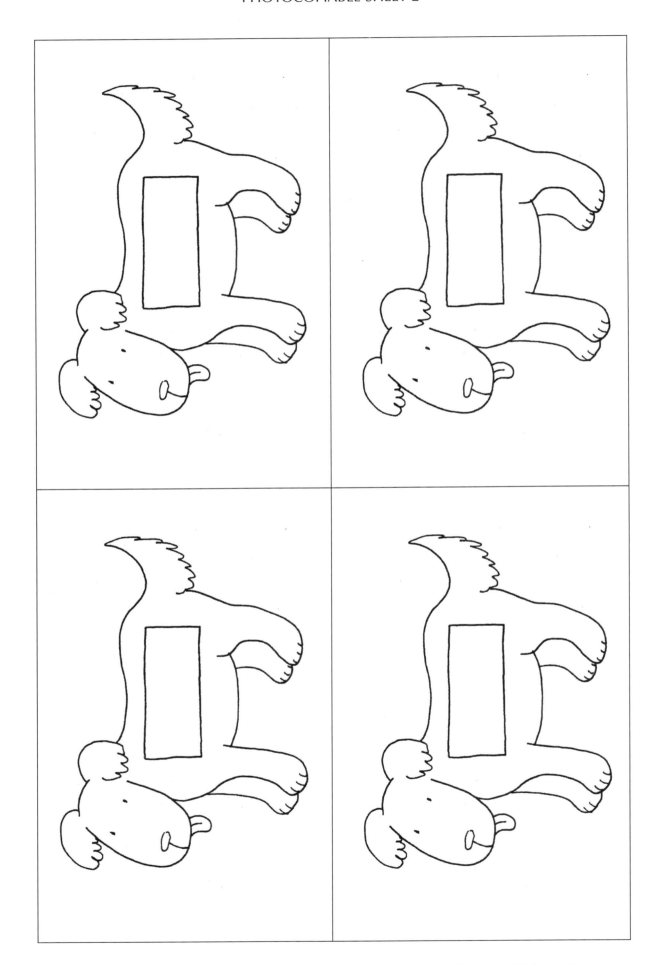

raindrops

lightning

hailstones

sunshine

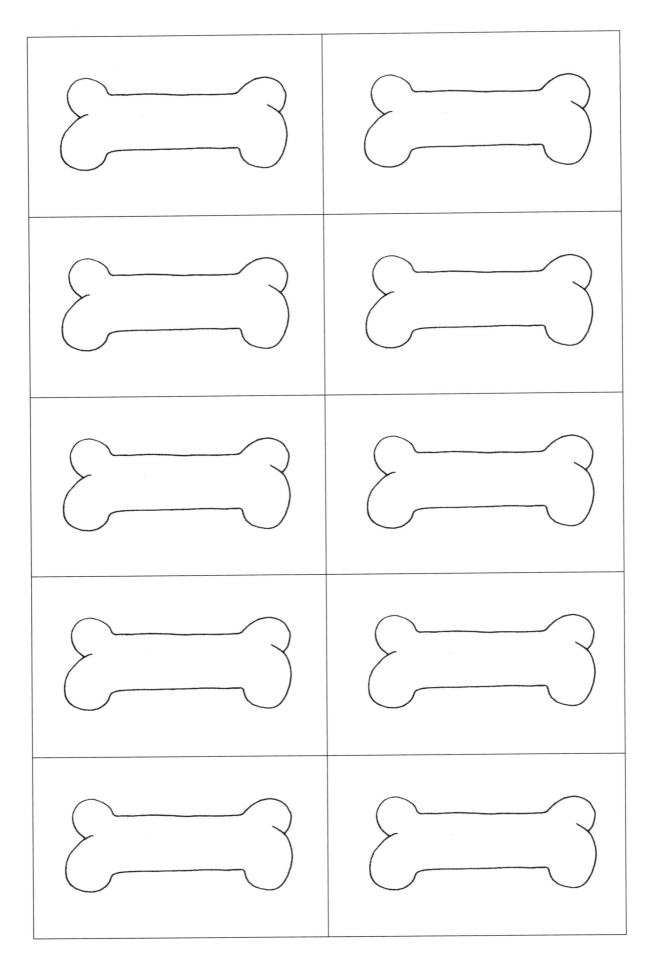

CHAPTER 3

Whiff or how the beautiful big fat smelly baby found a friend

by Ian Whybrow and Russell Ayto (Picture Corgi Books 2000)

Story synopsis

Whiff is a beautiful and well-behaved warthog, whose parents are very proud of him and want him to make friends and be happy. Unfortunately, every time Whiff tries to make a new friend, he comes home unhappy and in disgrace – he's either too rough or has bad manners, or is smelly, and the other babies' Mums just don't want him around. Poor Whiff and his parents are very upset and wonder who will ever want to play with such an antisocial baby. But everything turns out well in the end because Whiff pals up with Baby Littlebird who's delighted when lots of flies follow Whiff's smell – Whiff is a walking restaurant for Baby Littlebird, so the two babies play happily together, and both sets of parents are delighted that their babies' new-found friendship is so happy.

Early learning goals from *Curriculum guidance for the foundation stage*, Communication, language and literacy:

- Sustain attentive listening, responding to what they have heard by relevant comments, questions or actions.
- Extend their vocabulary, exploring the meanings and sounds of new words.
- Explore and experiment with sounds, words and texts.
- Know that print carries meaning and, in English, is read from left to right and top to bottom.

Objectives from the *National Literacy Strategy (YR)*:

- To track the text in the right order, page by page, left to right, top to bottom; pointing while reading/telling a story, and making one-to-one correspondences between written and spoken words.
- To reread a text to provide context cues to help read unfamiliar words.
- To know that words are ordered from left to right and need to be read that way to make sense.

Materials needed

- ■ *Whiff or how the beautiful big fat smelly baby found a friend* by Ian Whybrow and Russell Ayto (Picture Corgi Books 2000)
- ■ Rhyming family cards for Group A (see 'Preparation'; you might prefer to use your own or a commercially produced set instead)
- ■ Cassette recorder/player and blank cassette for Group A (optional)
- ■ Templates of flies and birds for Group B (see 'Preparation')
- ■ Card/sugar paper/coloured paper, as required for templates
- ■ Small containers (e.g. empty film tubs are good for this), variety of liquid scents or flavourings (e.g. lemon, chocolate, coffee, mint and so on – make sure you use things that won't harm the children if they taste the ingredient; avoid nuts in case any of the children have a nut allergy)

Optional materials for other activities

- ■ Books and toys based on a jungle theme
- ■ Materials to make a jungle in the Home Corner

Preparation

- ▲ Use Photocopiable Sheet 5 (p. 21) to make a set of rhyming family cards for Group A – stick the sheet onto card and cut it into the individual picture/word cards. (You could laminate them for future use and to protect from wear and tear.)
- ▲ Make copies of Photocopiable Sheets 6 and 7 (pp. 22 and 23) to make templates of flies and birds for Group B.
- ▲ Make copies of Photocopiable Sheet 8 – *There Was an Old Woman Who Swallowed a Fly* – (pp. 24 and 25) for Group C.
- ▲ Make up the different scents and put them into the small containers for Group D.

Introducing the text

- Look at the front cover of the book together and spend a few moments talking about it. Can the children guess what this story might be about? Encourage them to look at the picture on the cover to help them decide. Write their suggestions on the board to look at after you've finished the story. Read the title, tracking each word with your finger. Can the children guess which animal is the beautiful big fat smelly baby? Do they know what Whiff is? Have any of them heard of a warthog? Where? Point to the bird. Have the children ever seen one like this? Can they guess who might be the friend that Whiff finds? Point to the insects and ask the children what they are. Can they guess why the flies are swarming around Whiff?

- Look at the back cover and read the 'blurb', again tracking the words with your finger. What does it tell the children about the story? (That Whiff is always getting into trouble, and that he can't make friends very easily.) Can they tell you why Whiff might have trouble finding a friend? The 'blurb' says that everything turns out well for Whiff. Can the children guess why?

- Read the story to the children, letting them see the text and the illustrations. Track the text with your finger as you read, being careful not to lag behind or go ahead, i.e. point to each word as you read it. Stop from time to time (for example, when the flies come down or after the house has been wrecked) and ask the children what they think will happen next. When you have finished, ask the children whether they enjoyed the story. Can they tell you why or why not? Did it end as they expected? (Look at the ideas they gave you at the beginning of the session and see if they were right.)

- Focus on some specific things in the text. For example, talk about the different animals in the story – what do the children know about each of them? Why did Whiff get into trouble in each of their houses? Have a careful look at the illustrations and talk about what they tell us – how do we know that Mrs Crocodile and Mrs Monkey are angry? Is Mrs Littlebird angry too? How do we know? What is Whiff's face like in each of these pictures? What does it tell us about his feelings? Have a look at some of the words that the children might not know, such as 'disgrace', 'behaviour' and 'Jungle Monopoly'. Help the children use the context of the story to guess the meanings of any words and phrases they don't know. What do the children notice about the words used to describe Baby Littlebird eating up the flies? Can they tell you the initial sound and the final sound of each word? Can they tell you the difference between the words?

- Read the story again using intonation and tempo to put across the different moods in the story. For example, when the flies come down and chaos reigns, read the rhyming passages fairly quickly and with emphasis on words such as 'bashed' or 'snap' or 'whee'. Ask the children what they notice about these parts of the story.

- Can the children identify the rhyming words in these sections of the story? Help them to join in by reading each section and pausing before the rhyming word, so that they can provide it.

- Play a game where a child chooses one of the rhyming words and you all have to think of other words in the same rhyming family. For example, to 'bears' and 'chairs' you could add 'pears', 'stairs', 'wears', 'hairs', 'dares' and so on. Let the children think of nonsense words too, as long as they rhyme, e.g. 'gares', 'plairs', 'crares'.

- Have some fun reading the story again together, with the children joining in when they can – use expression and intonation to make it exciting and interesting for them (and yourself!).

Focus activities

Group A: Give the rhyming family cards to the children and let them play matching rhyme games. Can they think of new words to add to each family? (Let them use nonsense words too, as long as they rhyme.) They could either write or draw their new words or record them onto a cassette.

Group B: Help the children to make mobiles of littlebirds and flies, using the templates from Photocopiable Sheets 6 and 7. Alternatively, you could make a frieze or individual pictures. Help the children to write captions or labels for their work.

Group C: Share the poem *There Was an Old Woman Who Swallowed a Fly* with the children. Have some fun letting the children guess what the old woman will swallow next. Can the children add more animals before the old woman dies? Can they make up an alternative poem substituting jungle animals, including a warthog?

Group D: Let the children have fun exploring the different scents in the small containers. How many can they identify? Encourage them to explore what happens when they mix different scents – do they like their new odours? Why or why not? Can they make up some new words to describe the new scents? Let them write their new words, or scribe them for the children. Leave the scent containers for the children to explore in their own time.

Group E: Go into the garden and explore its minibeasts, including flies if possible. Help the children to observe and talk about the features of the insects, leaves, flowers and other natural objects during the 'research'. Make a model of a garden in the sand tray and put in models of the minibeasts you saw outside. (Don't forget the flies!)

Group F: Together explore some of the other animals that the children perceive as unlikeable or fearful, such as snakes, spiders or bats. Use the idea behind *Whiff* to make up a story showing the positive side of the animals or insects the children choose. You could use this opportunity to dispel any myths or misconceptions that the children may have about some of the animals they select, and to calm any fears or phobias they might have. Make their new story into a book and let them illustrate it themselves.

Other structured play activities

- Make a collection of books and toys based around a jungle theme, including some books about the insect life of the jungle, highlighting any that resemble the flies in *Whiff*. Display them attractively and leave them out for the children to explore on their own.

- Turn the Home Corner into the jungle. Let the children make the animals, trees and insects, etc., not forgetting warthogs, crocodiles, monkeys, littlebirds and flies! Help them to write captions and/or labels for their models.

- During warm days (if there's such a thing any more!) put some food such as a small piece of cheese on a saucer near the window, to attract flies. Don't use jam or sweet foods since this will encourage wasps – a child with a sting is the last thing you want. Together, look at the flies and talk about their wings, bodies, legs, etc. Let the children discover what happens if they try to touch the flies or go too near them. Can they tell you why the flies fly away so quickly? How do the flies know the children are coming near? Make sure the children wash their hands thoroughly after exploring flies or any other insects.

- When you're sharing other books with the children, make sure they know that in English we read from left to right and top to bottom. Do the children have the basic vocabulary and concepts of books, e.g. 'book', 'cover', 'beginning', 'end', 'word', 'author', 'illustrator' and so on?

- Use non-fiction books with the children to discover the life-cycle of flies. Use it as an opportunity to explain to them the importance of personal hygiene such as frequent washing of hands, especially after playing outside and before eating anything.

flies	eyes	pies
chairs	bears	pears
hat	cat	bat
pin	tin	bin

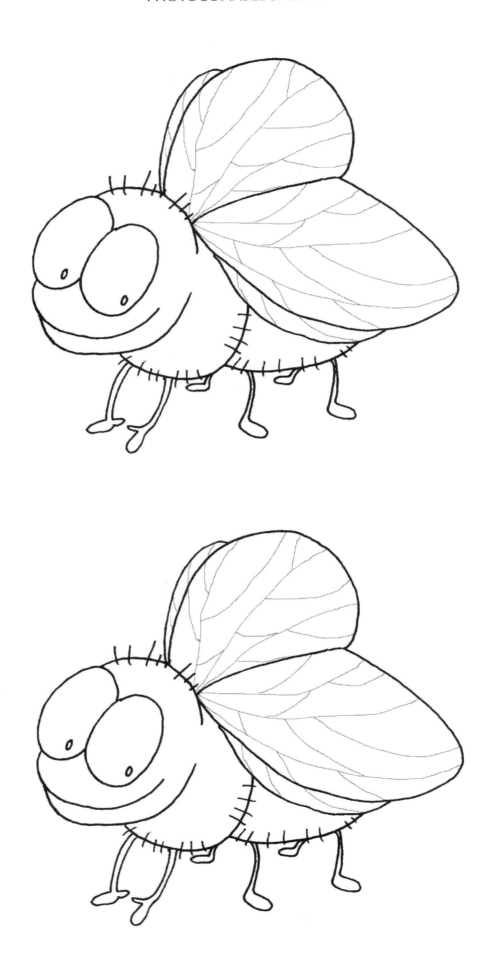

There Was an Old Woman Who Swallowed a Fly

There was an old woman who swallowed a fly.
I don't why she swallowed a fly; perhaps she'll die.

I know an old woman who swallowed a spider
That wriggled and jiggled and tickled inside her;
She swallowed the spider to catch the fly.
I don't why she swallowed a fly; perhaps she'll die.

I know an old woman who swallowed a bird.
Now that's absurd, to swallow a bird.
She swallowed the bird to catch the spider
That wriggled and jiggled and tickled inside her;
She swallowed the spider to catch the fly.
I don't why she swallowed a fly; perhaps she'll die.

I know an old woman who swallowed a cat.
Now fancy that – to swallow a cat!
She swallowed the cat to catch the bird,
She swallowed the bird to catch the spider
That wriggled and jiggled and tickled inside her;
She swallowed the spider to catch the fly.
I don't why she swallowed a fly; perhaps she'll die.

I know an old woman who swallowed a dog.
What a hog, to swallow a dog!
She swallowed the dog to catch the cat,
She swallowed the cat to catch the bird,
She swallowed the bird to catch the spider
That wriggled and jiggled and tickled inside her;
She swallowed the spider to catch the fly.
I don't why she swallowed a fly; perhaps she'll die.

I know an old woman who swallowed a cow.
I don't know how she swallowed a cow!
She swallowed the cow to catch the dog,
She swallowed the dog to catch the cat,
She swallowed the cat to catch the bird,
She swallowed the bird to catch the spider
That wriggled and jiggled and tickled inside her;
She swallowed the spider to catch the fly.
I don't why she swallowed a fly; perhaps she'll die.

I know an old woman who swallowed a horse –
She's dead – of course!

CHAPTER 4

Jack and the Beanstalk

by Val Biro (Oxford University Press 2000, Stories for Sharing Edition)

Story synopsis

This is a version of the well-known traditional story of Jack and his magic beans. It has been written with the idea of sharing the text in mind. There are refrains and repeated phrases for the children to join in, while the vocabulary itself is well chosen for developing the children's language skills. The illustrations lend themselves to discussion and exploration.

Early learning goals from *Curriculum guidance for the foundation stage*, Communication, language and literacy:

- Interact with others, negotiating plans and activities and taking turns in conversation.
- Sustain attentive listening, responding to what they have heard by relevant comments, questions or actions.
- Extend their vocabulary, exploring the meanings and sounds of new words.
- Write their own names and other things such as labels and captions and begin to form simple sentences, sometimes using punctuation.
- Use a pencil and hold it effectively to form recognisable letters, most of which are correctly formed.
- Read a range of familiar and common words and simple sentences independently.

Objectives from the *National Literacy Strategy (YR)*:

- To read on sight a range of familiar words.
- To learn new words from their reading and shared experiences.
- To use a comfortable and efficient pencil grip.
- To use awareness of the grammar of a sentence to predict words during shared reading and when rereading familiar stories.
- To think about and discuss what they intend to write, ahead of writing it.

Materials needed

- *Jack and the Beanstalk* by Val Biro (Oxford University Press 2000, Stories for Sharing Edition)
- Sheet with *Fee-fi-fo-fum* refrain (see 'Preparation'), a selection of plastic letters (upper and/or lower case according to your own aims), feely bag
- Musical instruments, sheet with *Fee-fi-fo-fum* refrain (optional; see 'Preparation'),
- Paper or card for leaves (either green or white to be painted, as required), paper, pencils or pens
- Sequence pictures of the story (see 'Preparation')
- Materials needed to make a giant-sized portrait of the Ogre, paper and pencils for Group E
- Rectangle of card fastened into a cylinder shape, card coins with required words written on them and with a paper-clip attached to each (see 'Preparation'), 'fishing-rods' with a magnet at the end of the string

Optional materials for other activities

- Clear plastic empty water/juice bottles, blotting paper, broad bean seeds, absorbent paper or paper kitchen-towels, water
- Large play apparatus (e.g. bench, slide, tunnel), items to represent the Ogre's treasures (e.g. a bag containing bottle tops for the money, a cuddly chicken and a wire cooling-rack for the harp)
- Old cartons, play dough
- Sequence picture cards of *Jack and the Beanstalk* (Photocopiable Sheet 10 on p. 31)

Preparation

- ▲ Make a copy of the *Fee-fi-fo-fum* refrain (Photocopiable Sheet 9 on p. 30). You could laminate it for future use. Put the plastic letters into the feely bag.
- ▲ Enlarge Photocopiable Sheet 10 (p. 31) and make enough copies for Group D. Cut them into the four individual pictures. You could laminate them for future use.
- ▲ Make a list of things needed to make a giant-sized Ogre, which will be checked against the children's later.
- ▲ Make copies of Photocopiable Sheet 11 (p. 32) and write on each coin a word you want the children to learn. Cut out the coins and attach a paper-clip to each one. You could laminate them for future use. Put all the coins into the upright cylinder on the table for Group F.

Introducing the text

- Show the cover of the book to the children and ask how many of them know this story already. Can they tell you the names of the main characters? Do they like the story? Can they say why or why not? Spend a few moments discussing the illustration on the front cover – who are the people in the picture? What's in the sack? Why is Jack pointing upwards? Why are their clothes patched? What sort of plant is beside Jack?
- Read the story together, pointing to the text as you read. Encourage the children to join in with the refrains such as *Fee-fi-fo-fum, I smell the blood of an Englishman; Lay, chicken, lay* and *Play, harp, play*. While you are reading, stop at appropriate places and ask the children to guess what word(s) might come next, for example when the wizard says to Jack 'I will give

you the beans, if . . .', or when the Ogre 'was tired, and he soon . . .' If the children suggest a word or a phrase that isn't exactly the same as the text, but still make sense, tell them they are right. Explain that we can use different words to mean the same thing.

- When you have finished reading the story, talk about it with the children. Do they feel sorry for the Ogre? Why or why not? Do they think Jack deserved his happy ending? Can they say why or why not? What do they think might happen to the Ogress after the Ogre disappeared? Can the children tell you why Jack's mother was angry when he brought home five beans in exchange for the cow? What does the author mean by 'And Jack and his mother lived happily ever after!'? Can the children tell you what Jack brought back home from the Ogre's castle? Can they tell you in the right sequence?

- Explore the text in more detail. Are there any words that the children haven't heard before? For example, do they know what a wizard is or what an Ogre or Ogress are? Have they seen a harp? Where? Do they know what it is for? When the Ogress says, 'Nonsense' to the Ogre, what does she mean? Can the children tell you an example of when we might say, 'Nonsense'? Point to the chicken's name (Chuckle) and ask the children whether they can think of any other names or words that begin with 'Ch', e.g. Charlie, cherry or chimpanzee. Have the children noticed the difference in what Jack's mother says to him on each return? ('You are a clever boy' first and 'You are a very clever boy' the second time.) When you read the story again, encourage the children to join in where they can.

- Look at the illustrations and talk about them in more detail. Focus on the facial expressions of Jack and his mother on pages 6 and 7 and ask the children what they think the characters are feeling. How do they know? Look at the facial expressions on page 10 – how do Jack and his mother feel now? How do the children know? How does the Ogress feel on page 13? What about her expression, Jack's and the Ogre's on pages 14 and 15? How do Jack and his mother seem to feel on pages 22 and 30? What about the Ogre and Ogress on page 25? What can the children tell you about Jack's mother's clothes from page 6, page 22 and page 30? Can they tell you why this change has occurred? What about Jack's clothes – do they change and if so, when? What do the children think of the food on Jack's table at the end of the story? Would they change it? If so, what would they put there instead? Why?

Focus activities

Group A: Give the group the sheet with the *Fee-fi-fo-fum* refrain and the bag containing the plastic letters. Play a game where the children take a letter out of the feely bag and say its phoneme. Then they chant the refrain, continuing with *I think his name might well be* . . . , supplying any name beginning with the letter taken from the bag. (You may need to help the children practise the additional phrase before you start the game.)

Group B: Give the musical instruments to the children and help them to plan and practise setting the *Fee-fi-fo-fum* refrain to music. Encourage them to interact, negotiate and take turns in the conversation. When they are confident in performing their piece, ask them to play it for everyone. You could extend it by using the longer version of the refrain on Photocopiable Sheet 9 (p. 30) and let the children add their own names each time they sing it.

Group C: Make giant-sized leaves to form a beanstalk going up the wall, if possible up to and along the ceiling. Help the children to write on the back of the leaves a sentence about their favourite part of the story. Put the leaves/sentences in the correct sequence as you make the beanstalk display. It's a good idea to photocopy the children's sentences beforehand and display the copies at child height, so they can be read more easily than those going up the wall and along the ceiling.

Group D: Give each child a set of sequence picture cards of *Jack and the Beanstalk*. Make sure the cards have been shuffled before you give them to the children. Ask them to put the pictures into the right sequence of the story. You might need to spend a few minutes talking about the pictures beforehand, making sure the children understand what each one represents. According to achievement level, you could ask the children to write a sentence for each picture.

Group E: Tell the children they're going to make a giant-sized portrait of the Ogre and they should make a list of the things they will need. Encourage them to discuss their list before writing it. When they are ready, help them to compare their list with yours. Let them collect the things they need and then help them to make their Ogre.

Group F: Let the children play 'fishing' for the Ogre's money. When they lift a coin with their fishing-rod, they should read the word on it. If they're right, they keep the coin; if not, it goes back into the cylinder. The winner is the child with the most coins.

Other structured play activities

- Grow some beans. Soak the broad bean seeds overnight in water. Cut the bottoms off the plastic water/juice bottles, to a height of about 15 cm (don't use glass jars for safety reasons), line them with the blotting paper and fill the centre hole with the absorbent paper or paper kitchen-towels. Place the broad bean seeds between the blotting paper and the jar so that the children can see them easily. Pour in enough water to make sure the blotting paper and the centre paper are wet – keep the containers well watered. Put them in a warm place out of direct sunlight and don't allow them to dry out. The children will begin to see some results in a few days. Help the children to label and write captions for their beans.

- Use the large play apparatus to set out a 'beanstalk route', e.g. across a bench, up and down the slide and through the tunnel. At the end of the route, place the items representing the Ogre's treasures. Play a game where the children pretend to be Jack and go for the treasures in the right order.

- Turn the Home Corner into the Ogre's castle. Make jumbo breakfast food with play dough. Use the chunky trowels and forks from the sand tray for cutlery, and make big plates from large sheets of paper or card. Use old cartons to make giant-sized furniture. Leave copies of the book in the castle for the children to explore in their own time.

- Enlarge Photocopiable Sheet 10 (p. 31) to make a set of picture sequence cards. When you share the story again with the children, give the four cards to four children and ask them to listen carefully to the story. When you reach the part shown by their picture, they should hold the card up for you and the others to see. Let everyone have a turn by giving the cards to different children each time.

- Let the children practise a role-play of the story, encouraging them to plan and discuss the format of their play. Let them dress up. Encourage them to use different voices, expression and intonation when speaking the different parts. Would they be willing to give a performance for a real audience?

Fee-fi-fo-fum,

I smell the blood of an Englishman

I think his name might well be ———————

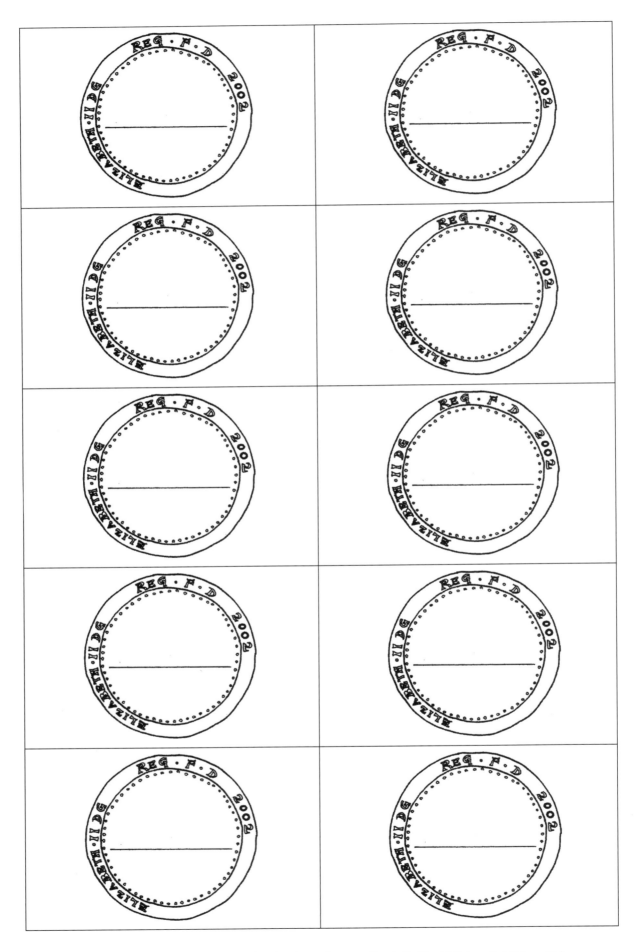

CHAPTER 5

Guess How Much I Love You

by Sam McBratney, illustrated by Anita Jeram (Walker Books 2001)

Story synopsis:

Little Nutbrown Hare and Big Nutbrown Hare try to express how much they love each other, and it isn't an easy job! As soon as Little Nutbrown Hare thinks of a way to describe his love, Big Nutbrown Hare manages to outdo him, until just as he falls asleep, Little Nutbrown Hare thinks of the ultimate definition – all the way to the moon. While Little Nutbrown Hare happily sleeps, Big Nutbrown Hare smiles to himself as he thinks of something that beats even that amount. But Little Nutbrown Hare will never know...

Early learning goals from *Curriculum guidance for the foundation stage*, Communication, language and literacy:

- Interact with others, negotiating plans and activities and taking turns in conversation.
- Sustain attentive listening, responding to what they have heard by relevant comments, questions or actions.

Objectives from the *National Literacy Strategy (YR)*:

- To use awareness of the grammar of a sentence to predict words during shared reading and when rereading familiar stories.
- To hear and identify initial sounds in words.

Objectives from the *National Literacy Strategy (Y1)*:

- To reinforce and apply their word-level skills through shared and guided reading.
- From YR to practise and secure alphabetic letter knowledge.

Materials needed

- *Guess How Much I Love You* by Sam McBratney, illustrated by Anita Jeram (Walker Books 2001)
- Flip-chart and marker pens
- *How Much?* cards (see 'Preparation'), tokens, a box, scissors, card, glue
- Hare templates (see 'Preparation'), card, scissors, glue, coloured marker pens, string
- The *Guess How Much I Love You* song (see 'Preparation'), musical instruments of the children's choice
- Draughtsmen and chequerboard, feely bag, plastic letters including l, n, h, w, s, r, t, m, f, b, d, u

Optional materials for other activities

- A selection of books about rabbits and/or hares – both fiction and non-fiction, cassette recorder/player, blank cassette
- Plastic headbands, card to make hare's ears

Preparation

▲ Make a set of *How Much?* cards by using Photocopiable Sheet 12 (p. 38). Stick it onto card and then cut out the individual cards. You could laminate them for future use. Put the tokens into the box.

▲ Make copies of the hare templates for each child in the group by using Photocopiable Sheets 13 and 14 (pp. 39 and 40).

▲ Type out the *Guess How Much I Love You* song (see Figure 5.2) in 14-point font and print a copy for each child. Have a selection of musical instruments for them to choose from.

▲ Put the plastic letters in the feely bag.

Introducing the text

- Look at the front cover of *Guess How Much I Love You* and help the children to read the title. Can they say, or show you, how much they love someone special? Jot their ideas on the flip-chart to look back at when you've finished reading the story. What are the two animals in the picture on the cover? Do the children know the difference between a rabbit and a hare? Explain that a hare is a bit bigger than a rabbit, its ears and back legs are longer than a rabbit's, it can jump higher and run faster than a rabbit, and it doesn't burrow like a rabbit but makes its nest, called a form, on top of the ground. Look at the frontispiece and spend a few moments talking about what Little Nutbrown Hare and Big Nutbrown Hare are doing. Do the children ever have a piggyback or shoulder rides with someone in their family?
- Share the story together letting the children see the text and the illustrations. Track the text with your finger as you read, being careful not to lag behind or go ahead, i.e. point to each word as you read it. Stop from time to time and ask the children what they think the Hares will say next. For example, when Little Nutbrown Hare says 'I love you all the way up to my toes!' what do the children think Big Nutbrown Hare will answer? Or just before the end, how will Big Nutbrown Hare outdo Little Nutbrown Hare's 'I love you right up to the MOON'? When you have finished reading the story, ask the children whether they enjoyed it. Can they tell you why or why not? Did it end as they expected? Did they like the ending?

Why or why not? Did the children think it was fair that as Little Nutbrown Hare went to sleep, he thought he had the last word when actually Big Nutbrown Hare had it? Do they think Big Nutbrown Hare ought to tell Little Nutbrown Hare when he wakes up? Can they tell you why or why not? Look at the ideas the children had at the beginning of the session, for how much they love someone. Were any of their suggestions similar to those of Little Nutbrown Hare and Big Nutbrown Hare?

- Explore the text in a bit more detail. Can the children explain why Big Nutbrown Hare is always able to go one better than Little Nutbrown Hare? Does it mean that Big Nutbrown Hare loves Little Nutbrown Hare more? Can they say why not? Why does Little Nutbrown Hare say 'Hmm' to himself? Explain to the children that this is something we sometimes say to ourselves or out loud when we're thinking about something and that it gives us a bit of thinking time before we say the next thing. What did this thinking time give Little Nutbrown Hare a chance to come up with next? Why does Little Nutbrown Hare wish his arms were as long as Big Nutbrown Hare's? Look at the part where Little Nutbrown Hare tumbles upside down to reach up the tree, and ask the children whether this is like the previous page where he was reaching up high with his arms. Can they tell you why or why not? How can Big Nutbrown Hare love all the way up to Little Nutbrown Hare's toes, and yet beat Little Nutbrown Hare's amount? Does Little Nutbrown Hare manage to add a bit to 'high' by hopping? How? Why does Little Nutbrown Hare want to hop as high as Big Nutbrown Hare? Do the children think that 'nothing could be further than the sky' or 'right up to the MOON', as Little Nutbrown Hare said? How do we know that Big Nutbrown Hare thinks he is almost beaten at this point? How does Big Nutbrown Hare have the last say?

- Look at the illustrations in more detail and talk about them with the children. Why is Little Nutbrown Hare holding onto Big Nutbrown Hare's ears in the first picture? Can the children show you the toadstools beside the tree trunk and on the next few pages? Have they ever seen toadstools? Does anyone know the name for all toadstools and mushrooms? (Fungi.) Can the children suggest how Little Nutbrown Hare could make himself seem to reach higher? For example, by standing on the tree-stump before stretching up. Do the children think that when Little Nutbrown Hare is upside down, he could have made himself longer? Can they say how? For example, that he could have stretched his legs to their full length. Can they see how Big Nutbrown Hare has added to that? Let them examine the picture carefully to see this. Spend a little time discussing the different poses of Little Nutbrown Hare on the pages that show him hopping around. How is Big Nutbrown Hare's hopping different from Little Nutbrown Hare's? Can the children see the difference between the lane and the river? How? Can they tell that Little Nutbrown Hare is tired? How? How do we know it has become night in the story? How do we know from the final pictures that Big Nutbrown Hare loves Little Nutbrown Hare very much? Do the children think that Little Nutbrown Hare is sound asleep? How do they know?

Focus activities

Group A: Use the *How Much?* cards to play a game with the children. Place the cards face down on the table beside the box of tokens. Each child in turn should pick a card and read the word on it (the picture should help the child to read the word). One of the other children in the group should identify the part of *Guess How Much I Love You* that is associated with the word. For example, if one child reads 'high', another one may say, 'Little Nutbrown Hare reached his arms as high as they would go' or 'Big Nutbrown Hare hopped as high as he could'. If the second child's answer is correct, he or she wins a token and the winner of the game is the person with the highest number of tokens at the end.

Group B: Have some fun measuring each child's arm span and height, getting the children to stand in the way that the Nutbrown Hares did. Depending on achievement level, use lengths of string to measure and compare these ('widest', 'wider', 'tallest', 'taller', 'longer', 'longest', etc.), or standardised measurements (centimetres and metres). Help the children to put their measurements in order and label them.

Group C: Give each child the hare templates and together make a group mobile. The children should write their favourite sentence from *Guess How Much I Love You* on the back of the template of Big Nutbrown Hare – you may need to help them with this. Let them refer to the book to jog their memories if they wish.

Group D: Use the hall or playground to play a game of *Guess How Much I Love You*, where the children imitate the actions of the Nutbrown Hares. Use soft mats if necessary. Call out the appropriate phrases from the story (see Figure 5.1) and encourage the children to perform the same actions that the Hares did. You can add an extra dimension to the game by telling the children to do the actions as fast as they can, with the last person to do each action being 'eliminated', until the winner is the last child left standing.

Group E: Help the children to put the words of the song in Figure 5.2 to the tune of *One, two, three, four, five, once I caught a fish alive*. Let them choose instruments to play to accompany their singing. Encourage the group to give a performance to the whole setting.

Group F: Line the draughtsmen along one side of the chequerboard, one piece per child. Let the children take turns to pick a letter from the feely bag and tell you what its phoneme is. They should then give you a word from *Guess How Much I Love You*, which begins with the letter they have chosen. For example, if they took out 'h', they could say 'hop', 'hare' or 'high'. If their word is correct, they move their draughtsman forward one space. The winner is the first to reach the other side of the board.

---

1. Stretch out your arms as wide as they can go.
2. Reach as high as you can.
3. Tumble upside down and reach up with your toes as high as you can.
4. Bounce up and down and hop as high as you can.
5. Run all the way down the lane as far as the river.
6. Run across the river and over the hills.

Figure 5.1 Phrases to use for the *Guess How Much I Love You* game

The *Guess How Much I Love You* song

(Sung to the tune of *One, two, three, four, five, once I caught a fish alive*)

Little Nutbrown Hare stretched his arms out very wide,
But Big Nutbrown Hare stretched his arms out even more!
'Oh, Little Nutbrown Hare, guess how much I lo-ve you,'
Big Nutbrown Ha-re says, 'This much and lots mo-re too!'

Little Nutbrown Hare reached his arms up very high,
But Big Nutbrown Hare reached his arms up even more!
'Oh, Little Nutbrown Hare, guess how much I lo-ve you,'
Big Nutbrown Ha-re says, 'This much and lots mo-re too!'

Little Nutbrown Hare hopped and hopped up very high,
But Big Nutbrown Hare hopped and hopped up even more!
'Oh, Little Nutbrown Hare, guess how much I lo-ve you,'
Big Nutbrown Ha-re says, 'This much and lots mo-re too!'

Little Nutbrown Hare pointed right up to the moon,
And Big Nutbrown Hare said, 'Oh, that is very far'.
Then Little Nutbrown Hare snuggled down and went to sleep,
Big Nutbrown Ha-re smiled. 'I love you there and back again.'

Figure 5.2 The *Guess How Much I Love You* song

Other structured play activities

- Leave a selection of books (fiction and non-fiction) about rabbits and/or hares in the Library Corner. Record *Guess How Much I Love You* onto the blank cassette and leave the cassette player and copies of the book in the Library Corner with the other books. Let the children explore the books and listen to the recorded story in their own time.
- Make some hare's ears and fasten them onto the plastic headbands (see Figures 6.1 and 6.2 on pages 46 and 47) Let the children wear the ears while they role-play the story of *Guess How Much I Love You* (or even at other times of the day!). You could also make scuts from cotton wool and add these to the costumes.
- If any of the children has a pet rabbit, ask them to tell everyone how they look after their pet. Make a collection of cuddly toy rabbits and have a display, together with books about rabbits and/or hares.

wide

high

all the way up

up and down

across

over

CHAPTER 6

Handa's Surprise

by Eileen Browne (Walker Books 1999)

Story synopsis

Handa sets out from her village to take a surprise basket of fruit to her friend Akeyo. There's banana, guava, orange, mango, pineapple, avocado pear and passion fruit. However, on the journey to Akeyo's village, Handa's basket, which she is carrying on her head, is gradually plundered by different animals that are tempted by the different fruits. As she arrives at Akeyo's village, Handa walks under a tangerine tree which drops its fruit into her basket, when a goat runs into the trunk. What a surprise both girls get – Akeyo when Handa shows her the unexpected basket and Handa when Akeyo says that tangerines are her favourite fruit!

Early learning goals from *Curriculum guidance for the foundation stage*, Communication, language and literacy:

- Interact with others, negotiating plans and activities and taking turns in conversation.
- Listen with enjoyment, and respond to, stories...and make up their own...
- Use language to imagine and recreate roles and experiences.
- Link sounds to letters, naming and sounding the letters of the alphabet.
- Write...things such as labels and captions...

Objectives from the *National Literacy Strategy (YR)*:

- To think about and discuss what they intend to write, ahead of writing it.
- To reread...stories with predictable and repeated patterns...
- To use knowledge of familiar texts to re-enact or retell to others, recounting the main points in the correct sequence.
- To sound and name each letter of the alphabet...
- To write labels or captions for pictures or drawings.

Objectives from the *National Literacy Strategy (Y1)*:

- To read familiar, simple stories...independently, to point while reading and make correspondence between words said and read.
- To write about events in personal experience linked to a variety of familiar incidents from stories.
- To make simple picture storybooks with sentences, modelling them on basic text conventions.
- To write captions and simple sentences, and to reread, recognising whether or not they make sense.

Materials needed

- ■ *Handa's Surprise* by Eileen Browne (Walker Books 1999)
- ■ The fruit featured in the story (i.e. banana, guava, orange, mango, pineapple, avocado pear and passion fruit), plate and knife for cutting up the fruit, bowl to make fruit salad in, bowls for the children who will eat the fruit salad, spoons, serviettes
- ■ Animal picture cards (see 'Preparation'), die (optional)
- ■ Fruit picture cards (see 'Preparation')
- ■ Plastic headbands for Group D. Card, scissors, glue, paint or coloured marker pens, to make ears, antlers, horns, etc.
- ■ Sheets of A3 paper for portraits, paint or coloured marker pens, pencils and paper for captions or labels
- ■ Zigzag books of Handa's animals (see 'Preparation')

Optional materials for other activities

- ■ Books featuring animals
- ■ Camera (optional) for supermarket trip
- ■ Materials for making animal masks
- ■ Feely bag and 'surprise' articles to put in it

Preparation

- ▲ Make animal picture cards from Photocopiable Sheets 15 and 16 (pp. 48 and 49). (You may want to write the initial phoneme at the bottom of each picture, or leave it blank, as required.) Stick the sheets onto card and cut them into the individual pictures. You could laminate them for future use.
- ▲ Make fruit picture cards from Photocopiable Sheets 17 and 18 (pp. 50 and 51). Stick the sheets onto card and cut them into the individual pictures. You could laminate them for future use.
- ▲ Make zigzag books by cutting a strip of thick paper long enough to make seven 'pages', one for each animal featured in *Handa's Surprise*. Fold the paper in concertina style, making sure the pages are equal in size. If you wish, you could write at the foot of each page 'The...ate the...' as appropriate. (If you choose to use the animal pictures on Photocopiable Sheets 15 and 16, make sure the pages of the zigzag book are big enough to take both the picture and the sentence at the foot.) Make enough for Group F.

Introducing the text

- Before reading the story spend some time looking at the front cover and discussing the picture. Can the children tell you where the story might be set? How do they know? Do they recognise any of the fruit in Handa's basket? Why is she carrying it on her head? What's watching Handa from the long grass? Read the title of the book – can any of the children guess what Handa's surprise might be?

- Look at the line of fruit inside the cover and ask which ones the children know. If you have real examples, talk about them with the children in terms of colour, texture, smell, size, shape, taste, etc. Let the children handle the fruit. When you have finished exploring the fruit, read the story to the children. Use a sheet of paper to hide the full-page pictures of the animals stealing the fruit so that you can focus on the previous page and ask the children what they think might happen next. Once the children realise the patterns of the story, the language and the illustrations, they should be able to predict the next bit. As you read, track the text with your finger, making sure you don't lag behind or go ahead, i.e. point to each word as you read it.

- When you have finished reading, ask the children whether they can remember what they guessed about Handa's surprise before you read the book – were they right? Why were there two surprises in the end? What was the surprise Handa received as well as gave? Did the story turn out happily? Would Akeyo have been quite as pleased if Handa had managed to bring her original choice of fruit? Why not?

- Look at the line of animals inside the back cover and spend a little time discussing them. Are there any that the children didn't know? Have any of them seen these animals? Where? Which is their favourite? Can they tell you why? Which is the tallest, the biggest, the fastest, the smallest, the shortest, the slowest? Do the children know the terms 'wild' and 'tame'?

- Explore the text in more detail. Can the children remember the names of the fruit that Handa puts in her basket? Can they tell you what she thinks about each one? For example, which one is soft and yellow? Or sweet smelling? Or round and juicy? Can they remember in which order Handa thought about them? Which fruit would the children like best if they had been Akeyo? Can they tell you why? Are there any words in the story that they're unsure about?

- Spend some time exploring the illustrations together. How are Handa's and Akeyo's villages different from the place where the children in your setting live? Encourage the children to think about the houses, the gardens, the plants and trees, the animals, the weather, Handa's and Akeyo's clothes and shoes, the way Handa carries her basket, the way the babies are carried around, how the food is stored, how the food is being prepared, and so on. Point out how each animal picture shows the previous 'thief' getting away with its loot, as well as the next one preparing its robbery. From this, can the children see the clue that it's the goat that will try at the end? Close the book and challenge the children to tell you which animals stole which fruit.

Focus activities

Group A: Use the fruits mentioned in the story to help the children to prepare a fruit salad. If you have difficulty finding all the fruit that Handa takes, you could use those that are available and supplement them with others that are in season. Plan with the group beforehand what you need and what you have to do. You could help the children make a recipe card for their fruit salad. Let the whole group enjoy tasting the fruit salad. (Check whether any of the children are allergic to any of the fruits beforehand.)

Group B: Put the animal picture cards face down on the table to play 'Animal Phonemes'. Each child turns over a card and tells you the initial phoneme of the animal's name. (You may have to explain that sometimes 'g' sounds as 'j', hence 'giraffe'.) Alternatively, place the cards face up and ask each child to point to a card that begins with a particular letter. As an 'added extra' to these games, you could let the children throw a die before they pick a card and if their answer is correct, they score the die-number they threw. You or the children will need to keep a tally of their total score to work out the winner.

Group C: Put the fruit cards face down in front of you in a pile. Play a game where you turn over a card and give the children clues about which fruit the picture shows, to help them to guess. For example, 'This fruit is soft and yellow' (banana). Let the children look at *Handa's Surprise* for support in guessing the more exotic fruits. Alternatively, you could put examples of the real fruits on the table instead of the cards.

Group D: Help the children to make some props for role-play using the plastic headbands. Cut out ears, beak, antlers, horns, etc. as appropriate and glue them to the headbands (see Figures 6.1 and 6.2). Let the children act out the story of *Handa's Surprise*, taking the parts of Handa, Akeyo and the animals.

Group E: Remind the children that Handa was taking a surprise to her good friend Akeyo. Encourage them to talk about their special friend – who have they chosen? Why are they so special? Where do they live? What would be a good surprise for them? Help the children to draw or paint a portrait of their special friend before writing a caption or label for their picture.

Group F: Help the children to make zigzag books of the animals that are in *Handa's Surprise*. Let them put one animal on each 'page' of the zigzag book. (You could either use Photocopiable Sheets 15 and 16 or let the children draw the animals themselves.) If you have written a sentence at the bottom of each page, help the children to complete them, either verbally or written, as appropriate.

Other structured play activities

- Look at other books featuring some of the same animals, for example *Dear Zoo* by Rod Campbell (Puffin Books 1984). You could extend the discussion about animals to pets and/or farm animals. Make a display of animal books, if possible with some models or toys alongside the books. Let the children explore these in their own time.
- Take the children to the supermarket to explore the fruit displays. Can they find any of the fruits featured in *Handa's Surprise*? Are there other exotic fruits there such as sharon fruit, star fruit, Ugli fruit, pawpaw, lychee and so on? If possible, take some photographs of the fruit displays to use in follow-up work back in the setting.
- Help the children to make animal masks for role-play. They could choose whether they'd like to be a wild, domestic or tame animal. Encourage them to invent their own story for imaginative play, involving all the mask-characters they make.
- Put some surprise articles in a feely bag and have some fun playing a guessing game, where the children take turns in feeling their surprise and deciding what it is without looking at it first. Some things you might put into the bag include a comb, a coin, a sock, an apple, a toothbrush, a toy car or a sweetie in its wrapper.
- Turn the Home Corner into Handa's home area, using the illustration in the book as a

model. Make the animals featured in the story and put them up around the walls in the order that they appear in the story. Have a real basket for Handa's fruit and make the fruits from play dough. (If you decide to use real fruit, make sure that it is removed before it becomes unsuitable for the children to handle.)

- Invite someone from Kenya, or a similar place, to come into the setting to share *Handa's Surprise* and to tell the children about life in his or her country. Find out if it's possible for the guest to bring in some examples of traditional dress, or even do some food preparation with the children.

Step 1

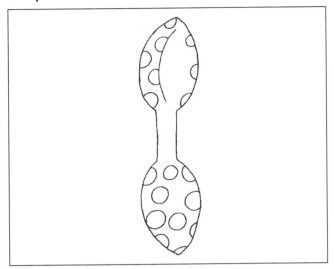

Fold paper in half
and draw required
outline plus 'bridge'.
Cut out, making sure
fold is not cut.

Step 2

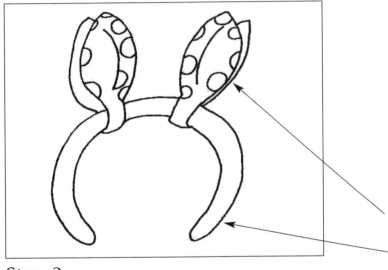

Wrap around
headband and stick
ears together.

giraffe's ears

plastic headband

Step 3

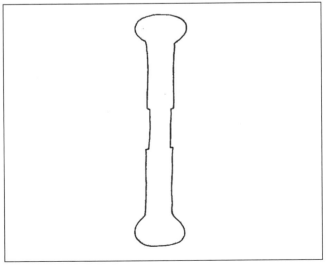

Repeat the process
for giraffe's horns.

Figure 6.1 How to make giraffe's ears and horns for role-play

Step 1

Fold paper in half and draw required outline plus 'bridge'. Cut out, making sure fold is not cut.

Step 2

Wrap around headband and stick top and bottom of beak together.

parrot's beak

plastic headband

Step 3

Repeat the process for antlers.

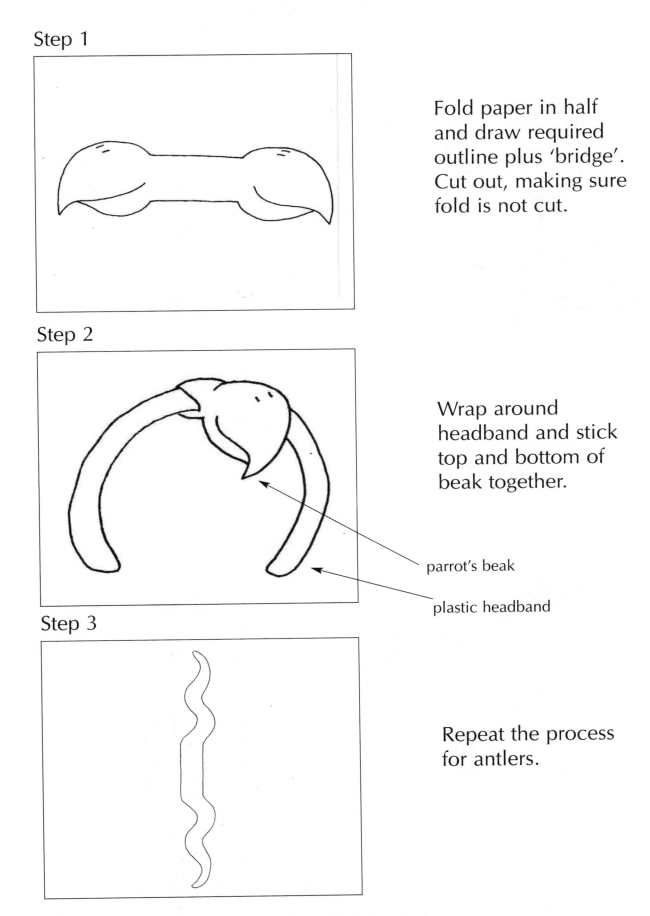

Figure 6.2 How to make antlers and parrot's beak for role-play

CHAPTER 7

Morag and the Lamb

by Joan Lingard and Patricia Casey (Walker Books 1992)

Story synopsis

It's spring and Russell and his dog Morag go to stay with Grandma and Grandpa at their house in the countryside. The sheep are in the fields and some of them are lambing. Grandpa warns Russell that Morag mustn't worry the sheep, and when the farmer says that dogs who do worry sheep have to be put away, Russell becomes a bit concerned. When Morag finds a lamb tangled in some brambles, she leads Russell to the place, to show him. The lamb looks very frightened and Russell's afraid in case Morag has worried it, so he calls the farmer to come and see. All turns out well, however, when the farmer explains what everyone means when they say that dogs mustn't worry sheep – and Morag certainly didn't do that!

Early learning goals from *Curriculum guidance for the foundation stage*, Communication, language and literacy:

- Extend their vocabulary, exploring the meanings and sounds of new words.
- Use language to imagine and recreate roles and experiences.
- Write their own names and other things such as labels and captions and begin to form simple sentences, sometimes using punctuation.
- Use a pencil and hold it effectively to form recognisable letters, most of which are correctly formed.

Objectives from the *National Literacy Strategy (YR)*:

- To reread a text to provide context cues to help read unfamiliar words.
- To read and write own name and explore other words related to the spelling of own name.
- To use writing to communicate in a variety of ways, incorporating it into play and everyday classroom life, e.g. lists...labels...letters.
- To use a comfortable and efficient pencil grip.
- To write letters using the correct sequence of movements.

Objectives from the *National Literacy Strategy (Y1)*:

- To read familiar, simple stories and poems independently, to point while reading and make correspondence between words said and read.
- To write captions and simple sentences, and to reread, recognising whether or not they make sense, e.g. missing words, wrong word order.
- To make simple lists for...reminding, etc.
- To develop a comfortable and efficient pencil grip.
- To form lower case letters correctly in a script that will be easy to join later.

Materials needed

- *Morag and the Lamb* by Joan Lingard and Patricia Casey (Walker Books 1992)
- Flip-chart, marker pens, string
- Generic Sheet 1 (see 'Preparation'), counters or tokens
- Turnips or swede, sharp knife (for your use only – see 'Preparation'), paints, trays for the paint, paper, overalls if appropriate
- CD that accompanies Book 4 in this series and CD player, animal picture/name cards (see 'Preparation')
- Photocopiable Sheet 20 (see 'Preparation'), the children's name cards
- Photocopiable Sheet 2 (see 'Preparation'), card, glue, scissors, black marker pen, laminator (optional)
- Copy of *Old MacDonald* (see Figure 7.1) or, if possible, the cube pop-up book edition, published in 2000 by Child's Play International, musical instruments of your choice

Optional materials for other activities

- Items to make the Home Corner into a farm
- A selection of books based on a farm theme
- Ingredients as required for food preparation or cooking session
- Photocopiable Sheet 20, cotton wool, glue, black marker pens or crayons, scissors (optional)

Preparation

- ▲ Use Generic Sheet 1 (p. 88) to make cards for Group A. Write on each card one word that has more than one meaning, e.g. *bat, play, break, wave, spring, plane, pipe, stamp* and so on.
- ▲ Cut the turnip into pieces large enough for the children to use for printing – squares or rectangles are the easiest shapes to make; mix the paint thick enough for printing and pour it into the trays.
- ▲ Make a set of animal picture/name cards using Photocopiable Sheet 19 (p. 58). (If you want to use cards without a picture prompt, use Generic Sheet 1 (p. 88) and write the name of an animal featured on the CD from Book 4 on each card.) Put the CD in the player and pause it at the animal noises track.
- ▲ Make enough copies of Photocopiable Sheet 20 (p. 59) for the children in Group D.
- ▲ Make two copies of Photocopiable Sheet 2 (p. 14), stick them onto card and cut them into the individual cards. On one set of cards write a noun in each dog's tummy and on the other set write a verb on each card. You could laminate the cards for future use.

Introducing the text

- Look at the front cover of the book and share the title with the children. Can they tell you who Morag might be? Help them to guess from the picture and the title. Point to the round yellow object with the brown spiral, which is towards the bottom left-hand corner – what do the children think it is? Have any of them seen a snail like this? Where is Morag standing? Have the children seen dry-stone walls? Where? If not, explain that they're around the fields in some parts of the countryside. How are the fields enclosed in your local area? For example, hedges, fences, palings, etc.

- Before you read the story, ask the children what 'worry' means. Can they tell you who might worry? Do the children themselves worry? What about? Do they know any other meaning for 'worry'? Read the story to the children, stopping at appropriate places and asking the children to guess what might happen next, or to tell you what they think about it. For example, when Morag first finds the lamb in the brambles, do the children think that Morag has worried it? If so, what might happen to Morag now?

- When you have finished reading the story, spend some time exploring the text in more detail. Are there any words or phrases in the story that the children are not sure about? For example, why is the farmer's tractor described as 'canary yellow'? Have any of the children seen or heard a canary? Where? What's meant in the story by 'a serious matter'? Can the children tell you anything else that we might think is a serious matter? Make a list of their ideas and spend a few minutes talking about each one. What does it mean when it says in the story that Russell 'turned pale'? Can the children tell you other things that happen to us when we're frightened? For example, our tummies churn, we feel hot and sweaty, our mouths go dry, and so on. When Morag was going down the garden, why was it she 'pricked up her ears'? Why should the lamb smell strange to Morag? Would it smell strange to a farm dog? Why not? What does 'eased aside' mean? Can the children tell you why the farmer eased aside the brambles?

- Ask the children again what 'worry' means. Can they give you more than one meaning? What does 'worry the sheep' mean? Do they think Morag worried the lamb? Why would the lamb look worried? Was Morag worried? Spend some time explaining to the children that we have lots of words that sound the same (and may have the same spellings) but they have different meanings. Can they think of other words like this? For example, 'bat' (the creature and the play equipment), 'play' (what the children do and something we see in the theatre or on television) and 'break' (to smash something or to have a short time away from a job or a place). Make a list of their ideas on the flip-chart and leave it up for them to explore. Leave a pen tied to the easel with some string and tell the children they may write on the list any other words they think of that have more than one meaning.

- Explore the illustrations together in more detail. What's the fodder in the farmer's trailer? Have any of the children eaten turnips themselves? Do they know the name for thorns? Ask them to explain how Russell is helping the farmer to feed the sheep (get the children to focus on the right place in the picture). What's the pink background to the illustration? What are the white bits at the top of the hills? Do the children know another word for these hills? (Fells.) Can the children suggest why Morag has put her head between Russell's feet when the farmer is rescuing the lamb? What does the lamb do when it rejoins its mother? See if the children can judge how the farmer feels from the expression on her face. Revisit the first illustration and the last one – what can the children tell you about them?

Focus activities

Group A: Place the 'double meaning' cards face down on the table and put the tokens in a pile in the centre. Get the children to play a game where they turn over a card and read the word. They win a token for each meaning of the word they can tell you. The winner is the person who has the most tokens at the end of the game. Let them play in pairs for support if they want to.

Group B: Give the turnip 'stamps', paper and paints to the children and ask them to make pattern pictures by dipping the turnip into the paint and printing onto the paper. Help them to write labels and captions for their pictures before making a display.

Group C: Give the group the animal picture/word cards (or the word only cards, if preferred), the CD from Book 4 and CD player. Play a game where the children listen to the animal noises track on the CD and then match the appropriate card to each noise they hear.

Group D: Give each child a copy of Photocopiable Sheet 20 and their name card, if needed. Ask them to write or practise writing their own name on the line in the lamb's fleece. Have some fun making up alliterative sentences with each other's names. (Make sure they are positive sentences to avoid sensitive children being upset.) For example, Susie – *Sweet Susie skipped slowly somewhere special* or *Michael managed to munch more marshmallows than Martin*. Scribe their sentences on the back of their sheets, or let them write them by themselves.

Group E: Put the dog cards on the table face down in two separate piles. Play a game where the children turn over one noun-dog and one verb-dog and then make up a simple sentence. The sentences can be silly as long as they make grammatical sense. Either encourage the children to write the sentences themselves or scribe for them. They could play this game verbally without adult support.

Group F: Have fun singing *Old MacDonald*, encouraging the children to join in, particularly with the refrains. If you have the Child's Play edition, let the children enjoy the pop-up pages as the cube unrolls. Help the children to accompany themselves with the musical instruments when they're singing. Give a class or setting performance and/or invite the parents in to listen.

Other structured play activities

- Together with the children, turn the Home Corner into a farmyard. Let the children bring in any toys they might be willing to share that are farm animals, e.g. cuddly lambs, hen and chicks, etc. Encourage them in their imaginative play, e.g. suggesting that tricycles are tractors, filling the trailers with 'turnips' (rolled-up balls of newspaper) to feed the sheep, and so on.
- Collect and display books, both fiction and non-fiction, on the theme of Farms. Leave them out for the children to explore in their own time. Also spend time sharing the books together in a relaxed and informal way, such as sitting with them on giant beanbags. Some suggested books on the theme are: *Farmer Doogie* by Peter Curry (Collins 2001), *Mighty Machines on the Farm* by Philip Ardagh and Tig Sutton (Belitha Press 1998), *Eye Opener Farm Animals* (Dorling Kindersley 1991), *On the Farm* by Jane Salt (Kingfisher Books 1990) and *A Day in the Life of a Farmer* (Franklin Watts 1997).

- Arrange a visit to a farm that is organised for and welcomes groups of children. It could either be a City Farm or a working country farm, according to your situation. Alternatively, you could invite a farmer into the setting to talk to the children about the job; a bonus would be a sheep farmer who brings the sheepdog in as well. Help the children to write the invitation letter or application to visit.
- Discuss what food we get from a farm, e.g. milk, eggs, cheese, butter, vegetables and fruit. Talk about the food that comes indirectly from a farm, e.g. bread, cakes and biscuits (wheat). Have some food-preparation or cooking sessions using some of these foods. Let the children eat the food they make in the Home Corner Farm. (Check for any food allergies and ask the child's parents for advice before you do this. Be vigilant of the children if you cook with anything hot.)
- Enlarge Photocopiable Sheet 20 and make a copy for each child. Give the children some cotton wool for fleece and help them to make their lambs. Make a display of the children's flock. You could expand it to a complete frieze showing a farm scene.
- Look at the words with more than one meaning that the children have added to the original list and spend some time talking about the different ways we can interpret them.

Old MacDonald

Old MacDonald had a farm, ee i ee i oh
And on this farm he had a cow, ee i ee i oh.
With a moo moo here and a moo moo there,
Here a moo, there a moo, everywhere a moo moo.
Old MacDonald had a farm, ee i ee i oh.

Old MacDonald had a farm, ee i ee i oh
And on this farm he had a horse, ee i ee i oh.
With a neigh neigh here and a neigh neigh there,
Here a neigh, there a neigh, everywhere a neigh neigh.
Old MacDonald had a farm, ee i ee i oh.

Old MacDonald had a farm, ee i ee i oh
And on this farm he had a pig, ee i ee i oh.
With an oink oink here and an oink oink there,
Here an oink, there an oink, everywhere an oink oink.
Old MacDonald had a farm, ee i ee i oh.

Old MacDonald had a farm, ee i ee i oh
And on this farm he had a dog, ee i ee i oh.
With a woof woof here and a woof woof there,
Here a woof, there a woof, everywhere a woof woof.
Old MacDonald had a farm, ee i ee i oh.

Old MacDonald had a farm, ee i ee i oh
And on this farm he had a hen, ee i ee i oh.
With a cluck cluck here and a cluck cluck there,
Here a cluck, there a cluck, everywhere a cluck cluck.
Old MacDonald had a farm, ee i ee i oh.

Old MacDonald had a farm, ee i ee i oh
And on this farm he had a duck, ee i ee i oh.
With a quack quack here and a quack quack there,
Here a quack, there a quack, everywhere a quack quack.
Old MacDonald had a farm, ee i ee i oh.

Old MacDonald had a farm, ee i ee i oh
And on this farm he had a cat, ee i ee i oh.
With a meow meow here and a meow meow there,
Here a meow, there a meow, everywhere a meow meow.
Old MacDonald had a farm, ee i ee i oh.

Old MacDonald had a farm, ee i ee i oh
And on this farm he had a mouse, ee i ee i oh.
With a squeak squeak here and a squeak squeak there,
Here a squeak, there a squeak, everywhere a squeak squeak.
Old MacDonald had a farm, ee i ee i oh.

Old MacDonald had a farm, ee i ee i oh
And on this farm he had a bee, ee i ee i oh.
With a buzz buzz here and a buzz buzz there,
Here a buzz, there a buzz, everywhere a buzz buzz.
Old MacDonald had a farm, ee i ee i oh.

Figure 7.1 *Old MacDonald*

dog

cat

horse

cow

sheep

cockerel

CHAPTER 8

Dear Daddy

by Philippe Dupasquier (Andersen Press 2002)

> ## Story synopsis
>
> Sophie's Daddy is an able seaman on a freighter in the Far East. For the year that he's away, Sophie writes to him, telling him about life at home with her Mummy and younger brother. The text and the illustrations track the seasonal changes and the difference between Sophie's and Daddy's days, and at the same time explore what it's like for Sophie to be separated from her Daddy.

Early learning goals from *Curriculum guidance for the foundation stage,* Communication, language and literacy:

- Use talk to organise, sequence and clarify thinking, ideas, feelings and events.
- Show an understanding of the elements of stories, such as main character, sequence of events, and openings, and how information can be found in non-fiction texts to answer questions about where, who, why and how.

Objectives from the *National Literacy Strategy (YR)*:

- To understand that words can be written down to be read again for a wide range of purposes.
- To learn new words from their reading and shared experiences.

Objectives from the *National Literacy Strategy (Y1)*:

- To become aware of character and dialogue, e.g. by role-playing parts when reading aloud stories . . . with others.
- To retell stories, to give the main points in sequence and to pick out significant incidents.

Objectives from the *National Literacy Strategy (Y2)*:

- To understand time and sequential relationships in stories, i.e. what happened when.
- To learn new words from reading linked to particular topics.

Materials needed

- ■ *Dear Daddy* by Philippe Dupasquier (Andersen Press 2002)
- ■ Roll of old wallpaper, own choice of white material for snowman (e.g. cotton wool), white fabric or small pieces of white polystyrene used for packing (make sure nobody's allergic to these), glue, scissors, black and orange card or stiff paper for eyes and nose
- ■ Paper and pens, toy medical equipment, dressing-up clothes for the doctor's visit to Timmy
- ■ Ingredients and utensils for chocolate cake (see Figure 8.1), microwave oven
- ■ A variety of books about modes of transport
- ■ *Dear Daddy* cards (see 'Preparation'), die with numbers on faces as required (see 'Preparation') or ordinary die, tokens or tiddlywinks in a box

Optional materials for other activities

- ■ Books based on writing letters
- ■ Water play container, old margarine and yoghurt cartons, Lego or other plastic bricks
- ■ A selection of different envelopes, both unused and old

Preparation

- ▲ Make two sets of *Dear Daddy* cards by sticking Photocopiable Sheet 21 (p. 65), onto card and cutting out the individual cards. You could laminate them for future use. If you want to use a die with numbers less than six, make one as required from the net on Generic Sheet 2 (p. 89).
- ▲ Collect the ingredients and utensils for making the chocolate cake (see Figure 8.1).

Introducing the text

- Look at the front cover and spend a few moments talking about the picture and the title. Where would the children come across the phrase 'Dear Daddy'? Have any of them received a letter? Can they guess why there's a ship at the top of the cover and some children playing in a garden at the bottom? What time of the year does the cover show? How do the children know? Look at the frontispiece – can the children tell you why there are writing tools in the picture? What's special about the envelope addressed to Sophie's Daddy? Why are there red and blue stripes around its edge? What does 'Air Mail' mean? Have the children seen a pen and a bottle of ink like those in the picture?
- Share the story with the children and as you read, track the text with your finger, making sure you don't lag behind or go ahead, i.e. point to each word as you read it. Pause from time to time (for example, after the leaves have fallen in the garden or when the snow is falling) and ask the children what they think might come next. When you've finished reading, ask the children whether they enjoyed the story. Can they tell you why or why not? Did they think the ending was good? Why or why not?
- Explore the text in more detail. Are there any words that the children might not know? For example, what are gumboots? What's a map? What's a stethoscope? What's a pianist? What

phrases in the book show us that Sophie misses her Daddy? ('I think about you lots and lots', 'We think about you all the time', 'I wish you were home again', 'When you come home, we'll do all sorts of things together', 'I know we'll soon all be together again', 'I think about you every day' and 'Please come back quickly'.) Did Father Christmas bring the bicycle that Sophie hoped for? How do we know? Can the children tell you what phrases in the story tell us that time is passing? (For example, 'school has started again', 'Father Christmas might bring me a bicycle', 'It's not long till summer'.) What does Sophie want to do with her Daddy when he comes home? How do we know that Timmy is growing? ('Timmy's got a new tooth. He's got six altogether now. Mummy says he'll soon be walking.') What are the main things that happened in Sophie's life while Daddy was away? (Her birthday, Timmy's illness, the repaired piano, her hopes for a bicycle and so on.) Which part of the story do the children like best? Can they tell you why? Is there any part that made them sad for Sophie? Why?

- Look at the illustrations in more detail. How can we see the changing seasons for Sophie? (For example, the leaves on the trees changing from green to autumn colours, the rain being replaced by wind and then snow, and the new leaves of spring then following on.) How are the changing seasons for Daddy shown? (For example, when he's on the ship dressed in a vest or at the port in Hong Kong wiping his hot head, then on board again in a storm at sea.) How do the pictures show the contrast between Sophie's life at home and Daddy's in Hong Kong? (For example, when Sophie and Timmy are building their snowman, Daddy is on the beach in the sun or in a Hong Kong market dressed in lightweight clothes; when Sophie's garden has leaves and flowers again, Daddy is being lashed by storms at sea.) Do the children know that the seasons are reversed on opposite sides of the world? Can anyone tell you why Mummy has such a miserable face in the snowman picture? Ask the children to guess what could happen next about the car – how do they know? (Five pages later, we see the bashed yellow car has been replaced with a new blue one.) Why is Sophie's duvet hanging out of the bedroom window in the springtime picture? In the picture where the bus pulls up outside Sophie's house, what does her face show? Can the children tell you what she might be thinking? What do Mummy's and Timmy's faces show? Do the children think we need more than just the pictures to finish the story? Can they say why or why not?

Focus activities

Group A: Help the children to make a huge snowman like the one Sophie and Timmy built. Get one of the children to lie on the unrolled wallpaper and draw around the child to get the outline. Fill in the snowman shape with the white materials. Make his eyes and nose. Help the children to write a label, caption or sentence(s) about the snowman.

Group B: Help the children to make up a role-play about Timmy's illness and the visit from the doctor. Encourage them to plan what they will need and help them to collect or make the props. For example, the doctor's stethoscope, the prescription that Mummy takes to the chemist (help the children to write this themselves), the medicine that she buys and so on. Let the children take turns in acting the different characters.

Group C: Make a chocolate cake like the one Mummy made for Sophie's birthday party. Help the children to read the recipe and follow the instructions shown in Figure 8.1. Make sure that none of the children is allergic to any of the ingredients and be vigilant of the children when hot things are around. Remind them to wash their hands before they start.

Group D: Explore with the children the transport that features in *Dear Daddy* – ships, junks, lorries, bicycles, cars, buses, vans, a pick-up truck and a dustbin wagon. Encourage the children to discuss who uses each form of transport and why. For example, the van used to deliver the repaired piano is different from that used to collect the mail, or the bicycle belonging to Sophie is different from those used by the tourists near the end of the book. Challenge the children to collect books about forms of transport and make a display.

Group E: Turn the Home Corner into Daddy's freighter and Hong Kong. Let the children look at the illustrations in the book to jog their memories about what Daddy did while he was away. Let them have free imaginative play sessions.

Group F: Play a game with the *Dear Daddy* cards, according to the children's achievement level. Decide beforehand how you'd like the children to score for their correct responses, either by taking a token, throwing the die you made (with low numbers) or throwing the ordinary die. Place the cards face down on the table and let the children take turns to pick up a card and read the word on it. They should then tell you something about the word, based on the story of *Dear Daddy*. For example, if they picked the card saying 'Timmy', they could say that Timmy was ill and had to have some medicine, or if they picked the card saying 'piano', they could tell you that the piano was brought to the house in a van. If what they tell you is right, they score according to your chosen method. The winner has the highest score at the end of the game.

Other structured play activities

- If you know of someone who serves on a ship, persuade that person to come into the setting and talk to the children about his or her job and life. If your town or city has 'adopted' a ship, help the children to write letters to the seamen on board.
- Look at some other books about writing letters, for example *Dear Zoo* by Rod Campbell (Puffin Books 2002) or *A Letter to Father Christmas* by Rose Impey and Sue Porter (Orchard Books 2001). Help the children to see that we begin a letter with 'Dear...' and end it with our name.
- Use the water play container to make the port where Daddy's ship is docked. Let the children look at the pictures in the book to jog their memories. They could use plastic blocks or building bricks (e.g. Lego) to make the skyscrapers and other buildings. Make the junks and ships from old margarine containers and empty yoghurt cartons. (Check whether any of the children have allergies, to avoid triggering a problem from minute traces of food.)
- Make a collection of envelopes, both unused and from old letters, and talk about them with the children. Show how we put the stamp in the top right-hand corner, how we write the address (look again at Sophie's on the frontispiece) and how we make the envelope secure by sticking it down at the back. Look at the different types of envelope and discuss what kind of letter we would use each one for. For example, air mail envelopes, 'Jiffy bags', A4 size, window envelopes, manila envelopes and so on. Help the children make an interesting display with the envelopes.

Chocolate Cake (microwave recipe)

Ingredients

125 g butter or margarine
125 g Demerara sugar
200 g self-raising flour

1 large egg
5 tablespoons milk
25 g drinking chocolate powder

Icing (optional)

125 g icing sugar
50 g butter or margarine

1 tablespoon cocoa
a little milk

Method

Line a 17.5 cm round dish with roasting film. Cream the sugar and butter together until light and fluffy. Sieve the chocolate powder and the flour together. Beat the egg and the milk together, lightly. Add the egg mixture and the flour to the creamed sugar and butter, a little at a time alternately. Beat the whole mixture well and put it into the dish. Microwave on High for six minutes. Allow to cool in the dish and then turn out.

Cream together the icing sugar and butter until smooth, then add the cocoa and milk to make a soft icing. Spread the icing on the top of the cake.

Figure 8.1 How to make a chocolate cake

Mummy

Sophie

Timmy

piano

snow

Daddy

birthday party

teacher

CHAPTER 9

Can't You Sleep, Little Bear?

by Martin Waddell and Barbara Firth (Walker Books 2001)

Story synopsis

Little Bear can't get to sleep because he's afraid of the dark, in spite of the lanterns that Big Bear brings him to light the bedroom. Poor Big Bear just can't settle to read his book because Little Bear keeps disturbing him. In the end, he takes Little Bear outside to where there's lots of dark, so that Little Bear can see for himself that there's no need to be afraid. Little Bear falls asleep in Big Bear's soft, warm arms because he's no longer afraid and Big Bear finally gets to read his book, right to the end.

Early learning goals from *Curriculum guidance for the foundation stage*, Communication, language and literacy:

- Use language to imagine and recreate roles and experiences.
- Retell narratives in the correct sequence, drawing on language patterns of stories.

Objectives from the *National Literacy Strategy (YR)*:

- To use knowledge of familiar texts to re-enact or retell to others, recounting the main points in the correct sequence.
- To write sentences to match pictures or sequences of pictures.

Objectives from the *National Literacy Strategy (Y1)*:

- To describe story settings and incidents and relate them to own experience and that of others.
- To re-enact stories in a variety of ways, e.g. through role-play.

Objectives from the *National Literacy Strategy (Y2)*:

- To use story structure to write about own experience in same/similar form.
- To secure the use of simple sentences in own writing.

Materials needed

- *Can't You Sleep, Little Bear?* by Martin Waddell and Barbara Firth (Walker Books 2001)
- Three boxes (small, medium and large), card to make thin tubes, yellow or orange tissue paper, scissors, red paint, paintbrushes
- Paper to make a book, pencils and coloured marker pens
- A variety of objects in big and little versions (e.g. big and little cars, 2D or 3D shapes, paintbrushes, dolls, books and so on), egg timer (optional), two labels – one marked 'big' and the other marked 'little'
- Story sequencing cards (see 'Preparation'), card, glue, scissors, laminator (optional)
- Materials to make a frieze of the forest at night and during the day

Optional materials for other activities

- Teddy bears, simple food as required
- Books and/or models of bears
- Cassette player, blank cassette, copy of the book (several if possible), a large sheet, a table for making a cave, cushions
- Four posters saying 'big', 'little', dark' and 'light' (you might want to have a picture on each as well), Blu-tack for sticking the posters on walls

Preparation

- ▲ Put the big and little objects in various places around the room, so the children can see them easily; place the 'big' and 'little' labels on two tables near where you will be playing with the group.
- ▲ Use Photocopiable Sheet 22 (p. 71) to make a set of story sequencing cards by photocopying the sheet and sticking it onto card before cutting it into the individual pictures. You could laminate the cards for future use. Make either one set for a joint activity with Group D or a set for each child, as you require.

Introducing the text

- Look at the front cover together and ask the children to guess what the book might be about. Does anyone have a lantern like the one in the picture? What about the little bear's cuddly toy? Read the 'blurb' on the back cover – are any of the children afraid of the dark? Can they tell you why? Look at the frontispiece and spend a few moments discussing it: Who might sit in the armchair? Why is there a basket of logs near the fire? What is the rail around the fireplace for? Can the children recognise anything on the mantelpiece?
- Share the story with the children and as you read, track the text with your finger, making sure you don't lag behind or go ahead, i.e. point to each word as you read it. Pause from time to time and ask the children what they think might happen next. For example, when Big Bear has brought the tiny lantern to Little Bear, what might happen? When he has settled Little Bear with two lanterns, what might Little Bear do? When Little Bear says how he's afraid of the dark outside, what could Big Bear do?

- Explore the text in a bit more detail. Can the children tell you why Little Bear isn't afraid during the day when he's out playing with Big Bear? How big is the lantern that Big Bear takes out first? How do the children know there isn't a smaller lantern in the bear cave? How big is the lantern that Big Bear takes out last? How do the children know there isn't a bigger one in the bear cave? What does the author mean when he says that Little Bear was 'cuddling up in the glow'? What does it mean when we read that Big Bear is 'padding' over to Little Bear's bed? How do we know that Big Bear is managing to read at least some of his book – can the children explain that we know it because there are fewer pages to go until the interesting bit, each time Big Bear is disturbed? Has anyone noticed how Big Bear's way of speaking to Little Bear changes through the story? ('"Can't you sleep, Little Bear?" **asked** Big Bear'; '"Can't you sleep, Little Bear?" **yawned** Big Bear'; '"Can't you sleep, Little Bear?" **grunted** Big Bear'; '"Can't you sleep, Little Bear?" **groaned** Big Bear'.) Can anyone say how Big Bear might be feeling each time? How is the last bit of the story clever – can the children tell you that the words 'THE END' are used both to finish the story and to mark the end of the book?

- Have a look at the illustrations in more detail. Discuss the differences between the picture at the beginning that shows the forest in the bright sunlight and the one at the end where the forest is shown at night: What can the children tell you about the two illustrations? What are the things on the mantelpiece of the cave? What is Big Bear's book about? Can anyone read its title? Explain to the children that 'Ursus' is a Latin word and it means 'bear' – can they tell you why this is a little joke by the author? (You may have to explain that Latin is an old, foreign language.) Look closely at the picture showing Big Bear's book when he puts it down for the first time – do the children notice anything about the illustration? Show them how it's a copy of the main picture on the opposite page. What do the children notice about Little Bear's cuddly toy as the story progresses? What can they tell you about how Little Bear's bedroom changes as Big Bear brings in more lanterns? Do they notice how we can gradually see more of the furniture and the toys? Do any of the children have toys like some of Little Bear's? What does Little Bear do to try to get to sleep? Do the children think his strategies would work? Can they tell you why or why not? On the page where Little Bear points to the cave's entrance, what is in the picture of Big Bear's book? Can the children see how it's copying the main illustration again? When the two bears go outside, is there anything to frighten Little Bear? Do the children like the picture showing Little Bear asleep in Big Bear's arms? Why or why not? What do the children notice about Little Bear's cuddly toy at the end? What do the children think of the pictures in this story? What do they think of the story as a whole?

Focus activities

Group A: Use the boxes to make some lanterns with the children – the tiniest lantern, a bigger lantern and the Biggest Lantern of Them All. Cut holes in each side of the boxes and paint the sides red. Make candles from a thin tube of card with yellow or orange tissue paper stuck into one end for the flame. Place a candle inside each lantern and secure it. Help the children to write a label, caption or sentence for each lantern.

Group B: Taking *Can't You Sleep, Little Bear?* as the model, ask the children to help you write another version of the story changing Little Bear's fear. Let the children decide what this should be and discuss how Big Bear could help him. Scribe the story for the children (their words) or help them to write it themselves. They could illustrate the story and make it into a class book for everyone to share.

Group C: Do some work on 'big' and 'little'. Challenge the children to collect items from around the room that show 'big' and 'little'. You could make it into a game by challenging the children to do this against the egg timer, for example 'Find me a big shoe and a little shoe before the egg timer runs out.' They should put each item on the table with the 'big' or 'little' label, as appropriate.

Group D: Using the story sequence cards, encourage the children to put the cards in the correct order and then retell the story in their own words. You could do this either as a group activity with one set of cards, or give the children their own sets.

Group E: Help the children make a large frieze in two halves, showing Big Bear's and Little Bear's forest both in the daylight and at night. Let the children look at the book to jog their memories about how the scenes look. Help them to decide what they need and how they're going to make the frieze. When they have finished, help them to write labels for each part of the frieze, for example 'moon', 'stars', 'sun' and so on. Encourage them to find the words in the text.

Group F: Look at *Can't You Sleep, Little Bear?* again and talk with the children about what (if anything) frightens them. Help them to make up a role-play using the story as a model but substituting one of their own fears for Little Bear's fear of the dark.

Other structured play activities

- Have a Teddy Bears' Picnic (indoors if the weather isn't kind enough). Encourage the children to bring in their teddies for the day of the picnic. Help them to do some simple food preparation such as bread and butter, and milk or juice, before having the picnic alongside their bears. Teach them *The Teddy Bears' Picnic* song (see Figure 9.1).
- Find books and/or models about other bears such as Winnie the Pooh, Baloo from *Jungle Book* or Teddy from *Andy Pandy*. Make a bear display and let the children explore it in their own time. Write some simple captions that the children can read themselves.
- Record *Can't You Sleep, Little Bear?* onto a blank cassette. Make a 'cave' by covering a table with a sheet, leaving the front open, and put the cassette player, the cassette, the cushions and the book (if possible, several copies) inside the cave. Let the children listen to the cassette and follow the story in independent reading.
- Put one of the 'big', 'little', 'dark' and 'light' word/picture posters on each wall in the hall. Play a word/picture-matching game where you and the children stand in the middle of the hall. You hold up a word/picture card and call the word followed by 'Go', and the children should run to stand near the corresponding poster.
- Turn the Home Corner into the Bears' cave. Let the children re-enact the story. Leave the book in the cave for the children to look at while they are playing.

The Teddy Bears' Picnic song

If you go down to the woods today you're sure of a big surprise.
If you go down to the woods today, you'd better go in disguise.
For every bear that ever there was, will gather there for certain because
Today's the day the Teddy Bears have their picnic.

Figure 9.1 *The Teddy Bears' Picnic* song

CHAPTER 10

Paddington Goes to Hospital

by Michael Bond and Karen Jankel (Collins Picture Books 2002)

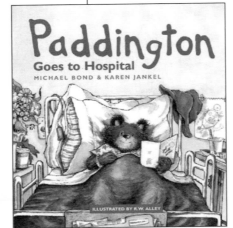

Story synopsis

Paddington has to go to hospital after he was found flat out on the lawn with no memory or even knowledge of what a bun is – there must be something seriously wrong! It's a learning experience both for Paddington, who has never before been in hospital, and for the nurses and doctors, who have never treated a patient quite like the lovable bear. After all the tests have been done, the operation carried out and a short stay on the ward, Paddington is deemed fit enough to go home but he'd happily return to hospital in the future.

Early learning goals from *Curriculum guidance for the foundation stage,* Communication, language and literacy:

- Use talk to organise, sequence and clarify thinking, ideas, feelings and events.
- Hear and say initial and final sounds in words, and short vowel sounds within words.

Objectives from the *National Literacy Strategy (YR)*:

- To use knowledge of familiar texts to re-enact or retell to others, recounting the main events in the correct sequence.
- To think about and discuss what they intend to write, ahead of writing it.

Objectives from the *National Literacy Strategy (Y1)*:

- To write and draw simple instructions and labels for everyday classroom use, e.g. in role-play area, for equipment.
- From YR to practise and secure the ability to hear initial and final phonemes in CVC words.

Objectives from the *National Literacy Strategy (Y2)*:

- To understand time and sequential relationships in stories, i.e. what happened when.
- To use diagrams in instructions, e.g. drawing and labelling diagrams as part of a set of instructions.

Materials needed

- ■ Black paper, white paint, brushes, water, picture of a skeleton (you can find this in *Funnybones* by Allan and Janet Ahlberg, Puffin 1999)
- ■ Patient cards and instrument cards (see 'Preparation'), scissors
- ■ Trolley, selection of empty bottles and containers (be careful not to use anything that contained substances that any of the children may be allergic to), paper, pens, scissors
- ■ Hospital sequence cards (see 'Preparation')
- ■ Syringes from water play, paint, paper
- ■ Boomerang cards (see 'Preparation'), feely bag, tokens

Optional materials for other activities

- ■ A selection of other stories about Paddington Bear
- ■ Materials to make a hospital in the Home Corner
- ■ Materials to make Get Well cards

Preparation

- ▲ Cut the black paper into the required size for each child. Mix the white paint thick enough to show up against the black paper.
- ▲ Make enough copies of Photocopiable Sheets 23 and 24 (p. 77 and 78) for each child in Group B. Stick them onto card and cut out the individual cards. You could laminate all the cards for future use.
- ▲ Make hospital visit sequence cards by using Photocopiable Sheet 25 (p. 79). Stick it onto card and cut the pictures into the individual cards. You could laminate them for future use.
- ▲ Mix the paints to a creamy consistency and pour one colour into each syringe.
- ▲ Make a set of boomerang cards from Photocopiable Sheet 26 (p. 80). Stick the sheet on card and cut out the individual cards. Write a phoneme on each boomerang, as you require. You could laminate the cards for future use. Put them into the feely bag. Put the tokens on the table beside the feely bag.

Introducing the text

- Look at the front cover with the children and ask them to help you read the book's title. Spend a little time looking at the picture together. Do the children think Paddington looks scared? How can they tell? Point to the call button and ask the children what it is. Can they tell you what the thermometer is for? Do they know its name? Who is in the drawing pinned on the wall beside Paddington's bed? What is Paddington holding in his hand? Have the children, or anyone in their family, ever received a Get Well card? What is the band on Paddington's wrist for?
- Look at the frontispiece and talk about the picture. Why does Paddington have something in his mouth and what is it? What is the nurse doing? Why does she have a stopwatch and a clipboard? How do the children think Paddington is feeling? How do they know?

- Share the story with the children and, as you read, track the text with your finger, making sure you don't lag behind or go ahead, i.e. point to each word as you read it. Pause from time to time and ask the children what they think might happen next. For example, when the doctor says he knows why Paddington's shoulder is hurting, can the children guess what the problem is? (Get them to look at the X-ray.) When the nurse gives him an injection, what will happen? When Paddington goes for a little walk around the ward, what might he see? When he keeps wheezing what might the problem be? When you have finished reading the story, ask the children whether they enjoyed it? Can they tell you why or why not? Did they like the jokes? Have any of them had similar experiences in hospital?

- Explore the text in more detail. Are there any words or phrases that the children don't know? For example, 'consulted', 'wailing', 'wheezes', 'complications', 'indignantly', 'announced', 'adjustments', 'whirring', 'socket', 'elevenses', 'patients', 'operation', 'observation', 'popular', 'appetite', 'temperature', 'pulse', 'tonsils', 'appendix', 'boomerang' and 'learning experience'.

- Ask the children to explain the jokes or humorous parts – two on the page where Paddington arrives in Casualty, two in the X-ray room, two when Paddington wakes up from the anaesthetic and one when Paddington is standing beside the little girl in the wheelchair. How do the children think Paddington might have felt at the different stages of his hospital stay? How do they know? For example, on admission, at X-ray, before the operation, when he came round, after dinner, the next morning and on discharge.

- Explore the illustrations in more detail. What do the expressions on the Brown family's faces tell us about their feelings? What about Paddington himself? Point to the serpent and staff on the ambulance door and ask the children whether they know what it is. Explain that it's the medical symbol that is recognised everywhere in the world. Can the children tell you the name of the instrument around the doctor's neck? (Stethoscope.) Do they know what it's for? What's unusual about the bed that Paddington is put on? Can the children tell you why it has wheels? Why is the radiographer wearing a green apron? What are the three things in the Casualty doctor's pocket? (A pen, a writing pad and an auriscope [or otoscope].) Can the children tell you what the auriscope is for? (Examining our ears.) Do they know what the blood pressure instrument is for? Ask someone to point to the instrument that gave Paddington the tiny prick. Do they know what it's called? (Syringe.) What is the letter on the X-ray of Paddington's shoulder? What does it stand for? ('Left'.) Why is it there? Explain that it's to make sure the doctor operates on the correct side, i.e. the left shoulder and not the right. What letter would be on the X-ray if Paddington had hurt his right shoulder? Why are the surgeons dressed in caps, masks and green suits? What are the big ceiling lights for? Can the children tell you what the monitoring machines are for? Why does Paddington have a mask over his face? Where does the tube leading from it go to? When Paddington is back in the ward, why does he have a tube leading from his finger? What are the charts at the bottom of his bed for? Why do some of the patients have a bag hanging from a hook near their beds? Can anyone show you the boomerang? What do the children know about boomerangs? Why did the medical staff rush up when Paddington blew his whistle – can the children tell from the picture what they would have done?

- Spend a bit of time talking about the pictures of the other patients and what's the matter with them. You could take this opportunity to look at issues of disability and serious or terminal illness, particularly if one of the children in your setting is in this position. Look at the little girl in the wheelchair and talk about physical disability. Discuss how some treatments for serious illnesses have side effects such as hair loss. When it comes to deciding whether to include these issues in your discussions, use your professional judgement and think about the extent or depth of your coverage. It's very important to talk about all these issues in a positive light, making sure the children don't develop either prejudice or fear.

Focus activities

Group A: Help the children to make some X-rays by painting a skeleton with the white paint onto the black paper. They should write a label, caption or sentence(s) for their X-rays according to achievement level.

Group B: Give each child a 'patient' card, and place the instrument cards face down on the table. Play a game where the children take turns to pick an instrument card and read what it says. They should put the card on the arrow pointing to the appropriate body part on their patient card. If the place has already been filled, they should put the card back at the bottom of the pile. The winner is the child who puts cards on all of the patient's body parts first.

Group C: Use the sequencing cards to play various games: (1) let the children sort the cards into the correct story sequence; (2) shuffle the cards and give one to each child. They should look at each other's cards and then stand next to one another in the correct sequence. The children should then tell the story in their own words, each child telling the part shown by his or her own card; (3) if you are sure that the children have a secure concept of sequencing, let them have fun making up a story out of sequence by placing the cards face down and turning them over at random. Tell the children that their story will be silly but fun.

Group D: Help the children to make a medicine trolley like the one in *Paddington Goes to Hospital*. Plan what each medicine is for, what it should be called and how it should be administered. For example, 'Juice for bad heads: drink one cupful three times a day.' Help the children to label the bottles and containers and to write the instructions for use. Depending on the achievement level, let the children write independently or scribe for them.

Group E: Let the children use the syringes with the different coloured paints to make some abstract pictures. Help them to write a label, caption or sentence(s) for their pictures.

Group F: Play a game with the boomerang cards where the children take turns to pick a card out of the feely bag and say the phoneme written on it. Depending on whether you're working on initial, medial or final phonemes, the children should tell you a word containing the phoneme. For example, if they take out a boomerang card with 't', they could say 'tin' or 'hat'; if they take out 'o' they could say 'hop'; if they take out 'sh', they could say 'shop' or 'wish', as required. If they're correct, they win a token before putting the card back in the feely bag. The winner is the child with the highest number of tokens at the end of the game.

Other structured play activities

- Have a selection of other Paddington Bear books available and leave them in the Library Corner for the children to explore in their own time.
- Ask the local GP to bring some medical instruments to the setting and show the children how they work and what they're for.
- Make the Home Corner into a hospital. Help the children to write prescriptions, charts, medicine labels, records and so on, for the props. They could either role-play the story of Paddington or have free imaginative play, as they wish. Let them use dolls, teddies and toy figures as patients, as well as themselves.

- If someone is away ill, such as a member of staff or one of the children, make some Get Well cards and send them. Let the children look at Paddington's cards in *Paddington Goes to Hospital* if their memories need to be jogged or if they want a bit of inspiration.
- If you want to explore the issues of disability, arrange for a disabled person to come to the setting and talk to the children about their day-to-day lives and how they manage their condition or situation. If you have children with disabilities in the setting, encourage them to talk about the implications for them.

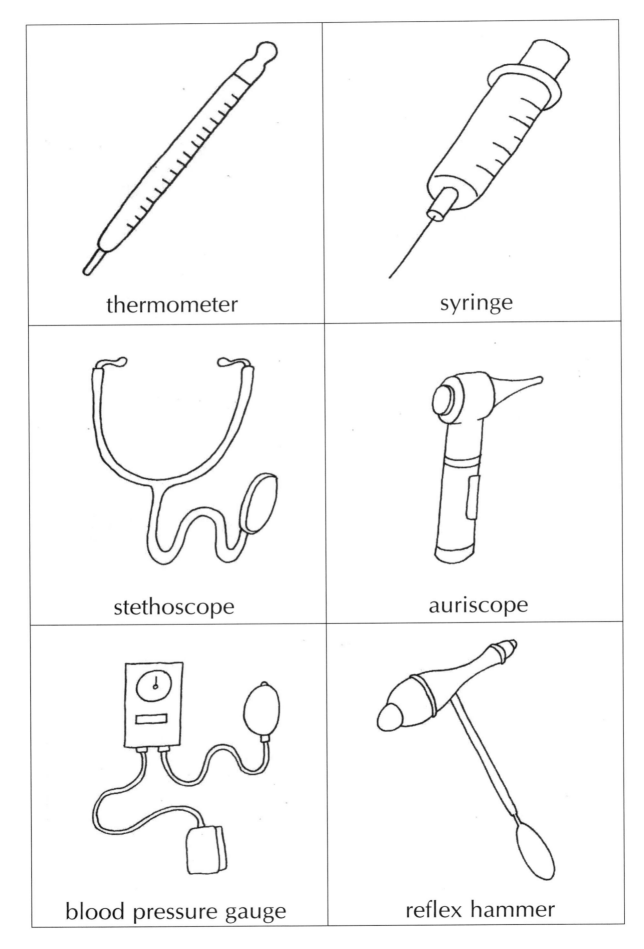

thermometer

syringe

stethoscope

auriscope

blood pressure gauge

reflex hammer

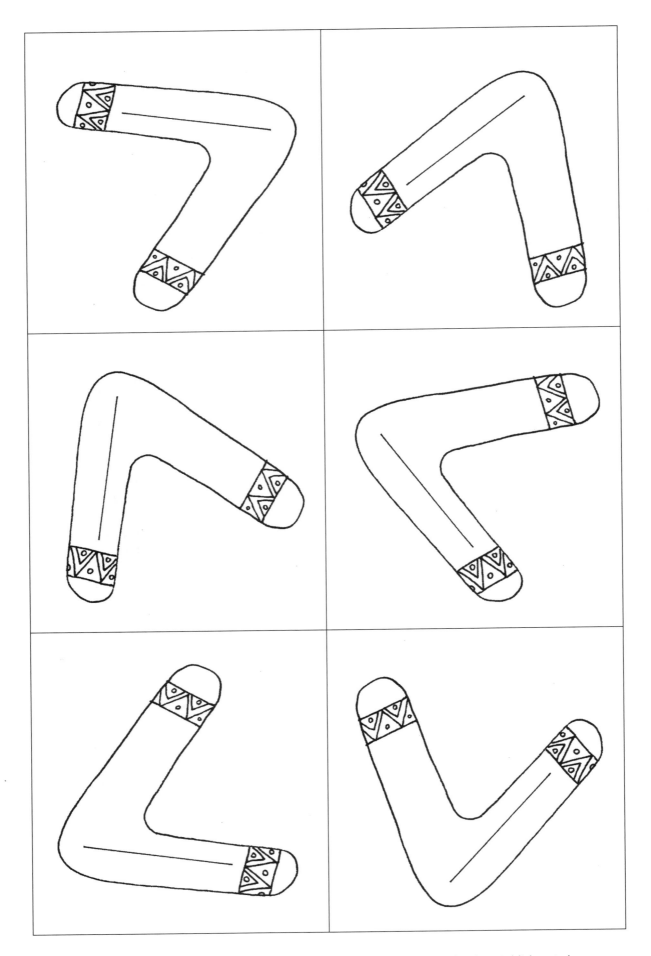

CHAPTER 11

A Letter to Father Christmas

by Rose Impey and Sue Porter (Orchard Books 2001)

Story synopsis

Charlotte accidentally sends her Mum's shopping list to Father Christmas, instead of her own wish list and so she has quite a surprise when she opens her stocking on Christmas morning. But in fact, the things that Father Christmas has left for Charlotte are exactly right, because she has been worrying about her animal friends out in the snow with nothing to eat. Charlotte's kind-heartedness is rewarded with a surprise at the bottom of her stocking – something that is perfect for a little girl who loves animals.

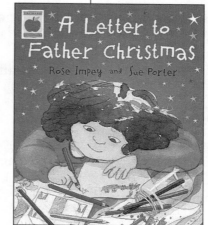

Early learning goals from *Curriculum guidance for the foundation stage*, Communication, language and literacy:

- Attempt writing for different purposes, using features of different forms such as lists, stories and instructions.
- Write their own names and other things such as labels and captions and begin to form simple sentences, sometimes using punctuation.

Objectives from the *National Literacy Strategy (YR)*:

- To understand that writing can be used for a range of purposes, e.g. to send messages...
- To use writing to communicate in a variety of ways...e.g. lists...letters.

Objectives from the *National Literacy Strategy (Y1)*:

- To make simple lists for planning, reminding, etc.
- To produce extended captions, e.g. to explain paintings in wall displays...

Objectives from the *National Literacy Strategy (Y2)*:

- Through shared and guided writing to apply phonological, graphic knowledge and sight vocabulary to spell words accurately.
- To note key structural features, e.g. . . . sequential steps set out in a list.

Materials needed

- *A Letter to Father Christmas* by Rose Impey and Sue Porter (Orchard Books 2001)
- Copies of the letter outline (see 'Preparation'), writing paper and envelopes, pencils or pens, stamps if required
- Animal/food matching cards (see 'Preparation')
- Rectangles of paper suitable for writing lists on, pencils or pens, coloured marker pens, coloured sugar paper for backing the lists for display, scissors, glue or staples
- Old envelopes with the stamps still attached
- Plain postcards or white card to make postcards, pens or pencils, flip-chart, coloured marker pens, balloons, inflation pump (available from good department stores or card shops), string, hole punch
- *What Do We Need?* cards (see 'Preparation')

Optional materials for other activities

- Large carton to make a post-box, red paint or red crêpe paper
- White paper, each child's shoe or wellington boot, pencils, mosaic squares of coloured paper, scissors, glue (unless you use sticky-backed paper for the mosaic squares), background paper for collage

Preparation

- ▲ Make enough copies of the letter outline (Photocopiable Sheet 27 on p. 86) for each child in Group A to write their draft letters.
- ▲ Make a set of animal/food matching cards using a copy of Photocopiable sheet 28 (p. 87) stuck onto card and cut into the individual cards. You could write the name of each picture on the line at the bottom if you want the children to read the words as well. If you'd like to extend the game, you could make additional cards by using Generic Sheet 1 (p. 88) for extra pairs of animals and food, e.g. dog and bone, monkey and banana, elephant and apple, etc. You could laminate the cards for future use.
- ▲ Make rectangles of paper suitable for writing lists on, cut backing for each list from the sugar paper.
- ▲ If you're making postcards, cut the white card into rectangles measuring 15 cm × 10 cm. If the children need writing guidelines, draw these onto the postcards. Punch a hole in one corner of each card and thread a piece of string through the hole. Write on the flip-chart, '*If you find this card, please write a letter to ... at X School, Address Lane, Kidstown, KD13 4CD*', filling in the details of your setting or school as appropriate. Inflate the balloons with the pump.
- ▲ Make a set of *What Do We Need?* cards by writing an activity on each card, e.g. going swimming, eating breakfast, playing football, painting a picture, having a bath, making a cup of tea and so on. You could add a small picture to the writing if the children need a bit of support. Choose activities that are within their experience and they would know what's needed to carry them out.

Introducing the text

- Look at the front cover with the children and before you tell them the book's title, ask whether they can guess what time of year it is in the story. How do they know? Show the dedication to the children and ask them what it means. Explain that sometimes writers put the name of someone special at the front of their books. Can the children guess who the Charlotte of the dedication might be? Tell them that from now on, they should look out for dedications when they read books.

- Share the story with the children and, as you read, track the text with your finger, making sure you don't lag behind or go ahead, i.e. point to each word as you read it. Pause from time to time and ask the children what they think might happen next. For example, when Charlotte's papers fell on the floor at tea time, when the animals had nothing to eat outside in the deep snow or when Charlotte opened her unusual Christmas presents. Can the children guess which animal would eat which present? When you have finished reading, ask the children whether they enjoyed the story. Can they tell you why or why not? Which part was their favourite? Why? Was there part of the story that made them worried? Which part? Why? Did they think the ending was good? Why or why not?

- Explore the text in a bit more detail. Can the children tell you how Charlotte is able to write even though she can't read? Have they ever copied grown ups' writing? Look at the little notes and samples of writing done by Charlotte. Does everyone understand them? Can they guess who 'Mr Pipes' might be? How do they know? Spend some time discussing Charlotte's letter to Father Christmas. Point out how her letter starts 'Dear Father Christmas' and finishes 'Lots of love,' and explain that this is how we usually write letters to people we know or can be friendly with. Talk about the things that Charlotte has written in her letter such as the instruction not to go to her bedroom, the directions for where she will be sleeping, the information about Ben being too small to write, the request for a surprise and the statement that she likes surprises best of all. Can the children make some suggestions about what other things they might write in letters to people they know in real life? For example, about things they're doing at school, about any trips they have been on, about things that have happened at home and so on. Focus on the envelope that Daddy helps Charlotte to write. Explain to the children that this is how we address envelopes to make sure the letter is delivered safely.

- Are there any words or phrases the children aren't sure about? For example, 'prowled', 'clutter', 'a strong draught', 'sparrows too dazzled by the whiteness' and so on. Do the children know what an evening class is? Does anyone in their family go to an evening class? Can the children suggest why Charlotte 'felt like bursting out laughing one minute and bursting out crying the next'? Have they ever felt like this? When? How did they get over it? Ask the children to tell you which of Charlotte's presents had 'sides which were soft and spongy' (the bread), which had 'a funny slopping noise' (the milk) and the one that 'had a funny smell' (the fish). Can anyone guess why Charlotte wasn't upset about her peculiar Christmas presents? Would the children themselves have liked Christmas presents like those? Why or why not? Do they think that Charlotte was pleased with the surprise present at the bottom of her stocking? Why or why not?

- Explore the illustrations in more detail. Look at the examples of Charlotte's copy writing with the children and ask them what the originals are (Mum's shopping list, an envelope, the plumber's note and a phone message). Why is Charlotte licking the envelope? Explain to the children that we need to secure our letters – can they tell you why? Ask the children why Father Christmas's room is full of letters. What can they see through his window? What are the nets for? In the illustration of the snowstorm, why do the animals look so unhappy? Why are there pictures of the animals in 'bubbles' above Charlotte's head?

Explain that this is how artists sometimes show us what someone is thinking. Have the children seen this anywhere else – for example, in comics? Is Charlotte pleased with her Christmas presents? How do we know this from the picture? Are the animals pleased with the presents? How can we tell? What was Charlotte's surprise present? Was she pleased with it? How do we know? Can the children tell you why Father Christmas is pinning Charlotte's list on his special notice board at the very end of the book?

Focus activities

Group A: Help the children to write letters, if possible to someone who means something to them and who would be willing to write back. For example, if it's Christmas-time, a willing parent may be prepared to reply from Father Christmas, or at other times of the year, the children could write to some of the older children in the setting or to children in another neighbouring setting. Spend some time helping them to plan what they are going to write in their letters and to do their drafts. Depending on their achievement level, you may have to scribe for them. If they are going to post their letters, help them to address the envelopes correctly.

Group B: Use the animal/food matching cards to play games. The children could do straightforward matching of pairs or play snap or pelmanism. Can they read the words as well as identify the matching pairs?

Group C: Together look again at Charlotte's list and how she has written it in columnar form. Explain that this is how we make lists. Help the children to write their own list of either Christmas or birthday presents they would like to receive. Let them illustrate their lists like Charlotte did. (If any of the children don't celebrate Christmas and/or birthdays, let them write a list of presents they would like for trying especially hard to be good.) Display their lists with attractive backings at child height, so the others can read them too. You could make the display similar to the notice board on Father Christmas's wall at the end of the book.

Group D: Make a stamp and envelope collection, asking the children to bring in envelopes with stamps on from their parents' old letters. Remind them to ask their parents before bringing them in. How many different places do the letters come from? Show the children how to identify where and when the letters were posted by looking at the frank.

Group E: Show the postcards to the children and explain that this is another, shorter way of writing to someone, if we don't need to write a letter. Spend a few minutes talking about holiday postcards too. Help the children to fill in their postcards using the sentence on the flip-chart as a model. If the children want to write their own version, help them to do this. Tie the postcards onto the inflated balloons. Take the children outside and let them release their balloons.

Group F: Place the *What Do We Need?* cards face down on the table and let the children play a game by taking turns to pick a card and read what it says. They should then list everything they think would be needed to carry out the activity on the card. If they're right, they keep the card; if they say something that isn't needed for the activity, they put the card back at the bottom of the pile. The winner has the most cards at the end of the game.

Other structured play activities

- Make a post-box using a large carton with a slit cut into it for the letters to be posted through. Paint it red or cover it with red crêpe paper. Encourage the children to write letters to each other or, if it's the Christmas season, to Father Christmas.
- Play *Grandma Went to Market* where the children have to make up Grandma's shopping list, either verbally or in writing, as you prefer and according to the children's achievement level. Let the children choose whatever goods they like for Grandma. Alternatively, you could add an extra challenge by limiting the children to only one phoneme for Grandma's goods, or by adding the goods in alphabetical order, again according to achievement level.
- Arrange a visit to the local Post Office and/or sorting office so the children can see what happens to a letter after they have posted it. Ask the school's postman/postwoman to come into the setting and tell the children about his/her job.
- Look at the footprints in the snow in *A Letter to Father Christmas* when Charlotte opens her bedroom curtains and when she goes out to feed the animals. Talk about the shapes made by the different animals. Can the children suggest what the cat's footprints might look like? Help the children to make some footprints of their own by drawing around their shoes or wellington boots and cutting out the shapes. Let them fill in the footprints with mosaic squares of coloured paper. Make a large collage with all the prints. The children should write a label, caption or sentence(s) to go with their designs.

....

....

....

Dear ....

_____

_____

_____

_____

_____

_____

_____

Lots of love from

_____

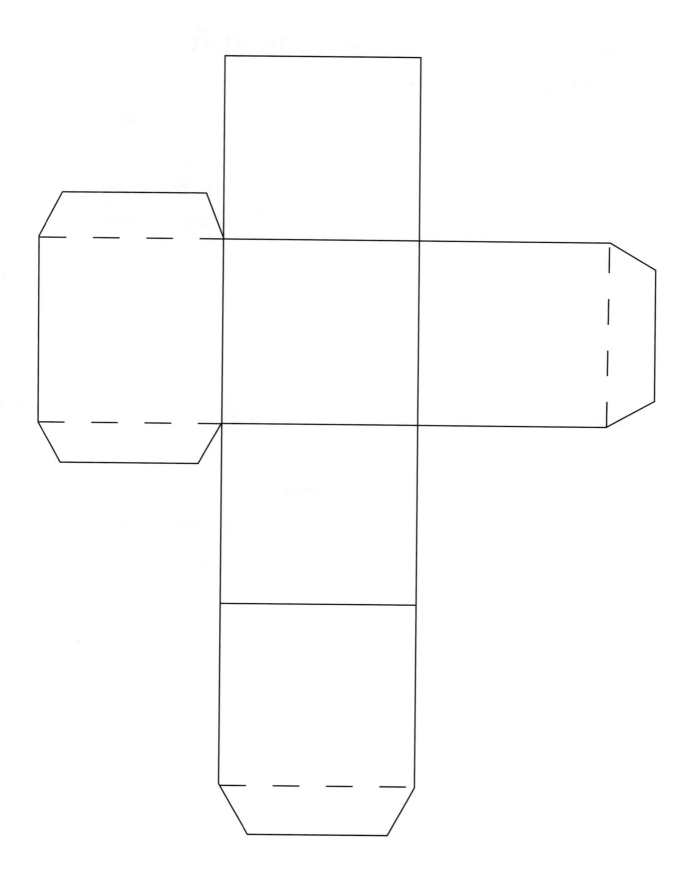

Observation and assessment for speaking and listening

During your sessions observing the children, you may find it useful to refer to some of these questions as a way of focusing on how their speaking and listening skills are developing:

- Do all children make a contribution to the whole-group or small-group discussion?
- Are the grammatical structures correct? Is the syntax correct?
- Do the children use appropriate vocabulary? Do they use context to work out unfamiliar words?
- Do the children show a curiosity about new words and try to explore how to use them appropriately?
- Is their speech fluent and clear?
- Do the children sustain attention when listening?
- Do they listen with respect to others' views and opinions?
- Do the children take turns in conversations?
- Do they appear to understand what is being said by you and by the other children?
- Do the children ask relevant and appropriate questions about a shared text?
- Do the children have a concept of the sequence of a story?
- Do they use the illustrations for clues about the meaning, sequence and content of the story?
- Do the children talk about key events and characters in a familiar story?
- Are they able to negotiate plans and roles?
- Do they enjoy listening to stories, rhymes and songs, and are they able to respond to them, taking part and using them in their play and learning?
- Do the children use language in their imaginative play? Do they role-play and create imaginary experiences?

Observation and assessment for reading and writing

During your sessions observing the children, you may find it useful to refer to some of these questions as a way of focusing on how their reading and writing skills are developing:

- Can the children hear and say initial and final sounds in words? Can they hear and say short vowel sounds within words?
- Can the children name and sound the letters of the alphabet?
- Do the children know that print in English is read from left to right, and from top to bottom?
- Do the children enjoy exploring and experimenting with sounds, words and texts?
- Do they have a knowledge of the vocabulary of literacy, such as 'book', 'cover', 'page', 'line', 'title', 'author', 'front', 'back', 'word', 'reading', 'writing', etc.?
- Can the children write their own name?
- Do they attempt to write for different purposes, such as letters, lists, instructions, stories, etc.?
- Do the children use their knowledge of phonics to attempt to read or write simple regular words?
- Can they hold and use a pencil appropriately?
- Do they write letters using the correct sequence of movements?
- Can the children recognise the important elements of words such as shape, length and common spelling patterns?
- Do the children use different cues when reading, e.g. their knowledge of a story, context, illustrations, syntax, etc?
- Can they identify significant parts of a text, e.g. captions, characters' names, chants, etc.?
- Are the children aware of the structure of a story, i.e. a beginning, a middle and an end? Are they aware of the actions and consequences within a story?
- Do the children check text for sense? Do they self-correct when something they read does not make sense?
- Can the children identify patterns in stories and poems? Can they extend them?
- Can the children match phonemes to graphemes? Can they write them?
- Do they understand alphabetical order?
- Can the children sight-read familiar words such as captions or high frequency words?